LIVING FEARLESS

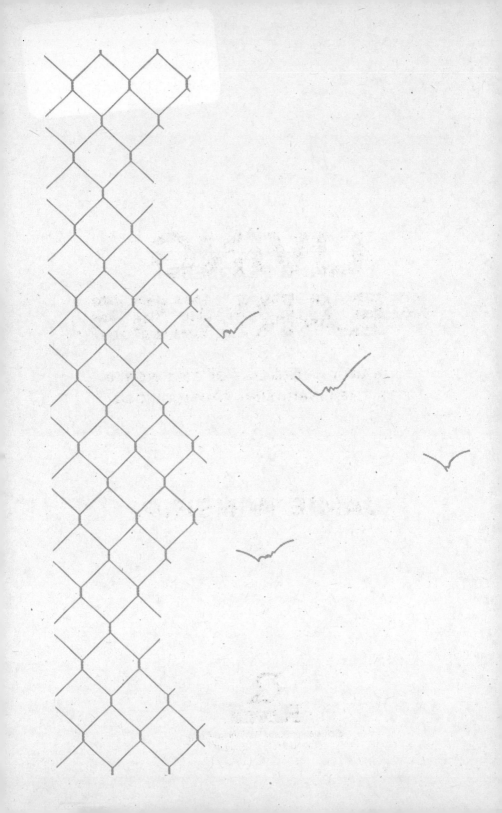

LIVING
FEARLESS

EXCHANGING THE LIES OF THE WORLD
FOR THE LIBERATING TRUTH OF GOD

JAMIE WINSHIP

Revell

a division of Baker Publishing Group
Grand Rapids, Michigan

Published by Revell
a division of Baker Publishing Group
Grand Rapids, Michigan
www.revellbooks.com

Printed in the United States of America

Library of Congress Cataloging-in-Publication Data
Names: Winship, Jamie, 1959– author.
Title: Living fearless : exchanging the lies of the world for the liberating truth of God / Jamie Winship.
Description: Grand Rapids, MI : Revell, a division of Baker Publishing Group, [2022] | Includes bibliographical references.
Identifiers: LCCN 2021041396 | ISBN 9780800740290 | ISBN 9780800741969 (casebound) | ISBN 9781493436378 (ebook)
Subjects: LCSH: Truth—Religious aspects—Christianity | Truthfulness and falsehood—Religious aspects—Christianity.
Classification: LCC BT50.W477 2022 | DDC 231/.042—dc23
LC record available at https://lccn.loc.gov/2021041396

Unless otherwise indicated, Scripture quotations are from the Amplified® Bible (AMPC), copyright © 1954, 1958, 1962, 1964, 1965, 1987 by The Lockman Foundation. Used by permission. www.Lockman.org

Scripture quotations labeled AMP are from the Amplified® Bible (AMP), copyright © 2015 by The Lockman Foundation. Used by permission. www.Lockman.org

Scripture quotations labeled ERV are from the HOLY BIBLE: EASY-TO-READ VERSION © 2014 by Bible League International. Used by permission.

Scripture quotations labeled ESV are from The Holy Bible, English Standard Version® (ESV®), copyright © 2001 by Crossway, a publishing ministry of Good News Publishers. Used by permission. All rights reserved. ESV Text Edition: 2016

Scripture quotations labeled KJV are from the King James Version of the Bible.

Scripture quotations labeled MSG are from THE MESSAGE, copyright © 1993, 2002, 2018 by Eugene H. Peterson. Used by permission of NavPress. All rights reserved. Represented by Tyndale House Publishers, Inc.

Scripture quotations labeled NASB are from the (NASB®) New American Standard Bible®, Copyright © 1960, 1971, 1977, 1995, 2020 by The Lockman Foundation. Used by permission. All rights reserved. www.lockman.org

Scripture quotations labeled NIV are from THE HOLY BIBLE, NEW INTERNATIONAL VERSION®, NIV® Copyright © 1973, 1978, 1984, 2011 by Biblica, Inc.® Used by permission. All rights reserved worldwide.

Scripture quotations labeled NKJV are from the New King James Version®. Copyright © 1982 by Thomas Nelson. Used by permission. All rights reserved.

Scripture quotations labeled NLT are from the Holy Bible, New Living Translation, copyright © 1996, 2004, 2007, 2013, 2015 by Tyndale House Foundation. Used by permission of Tyndale House Publishers, Inc., Carol Stream, Illinois 60188. All rights reserved.

Scripture quotations labeled TPT are from The Passion Translation®. Copyright © 2017, 2018 by Passion & Fire Ministries, Inc. Used by permission. All rights reserved. ThePassionTranslation.com.

Scripture quotations labeled WE are from the Worldwide English (New Testament) (WE) © 1969, 1971, 1996, 1998 by SOON Educational Publications.

The names and details of the people and situations described in this book have been changed or presented in composite form in order to ensure the privacy of those with whom the author has worked.

Baker Publishing Group publications use paper produced from sustainable forestry practices and post-consumer waste whenever possible.

24   25   26   27   28   29   15   14   13   12   11

This is for Mac,
who taught me, like Tennyson's *Ulysses*,
that "I am a part of all that I have met."

Contents

Preface

"This is total nonsense!"

That's how a doctoral-level midwife responded when I asked her to close her eyes and allow herself to receive an understanding of her true identity instead of the various false identities that were negatively affecting her in the present.

She was one of thirteen midwives taking part in a professional-development day focused on true identity versus false identity and its effect on team dynamics in the workplace.

We were sitting in a circle, working through the exercise, but this doctor was not about to continue. The other midwives, all highly educated and experienced professionals, stared at me for direction. Honestly, I felt like telling them to take a ten-minute break, slinking away to my car, and driving off.

For some reason, this group of midwives was more intimidating to me than the group of Muslim nomads that Art (nmn) Blumfield[1] and I led through this very same process in the middle of the Sahara Desert during my training years. They had threatened that if the identity-exchange process didn't transform their thinking dramatically, they would "get rid of us" and join the extremist militant organization trying to recruit them. Our goal was to prevent both of those things.

"This isn't good, Art," I whispered. "They don't look happy."

"Have faith," Art said in his irritatingly calm manner.

"These guys are freaking out," I rasped, imagining my wife and kids at my graveside.

Art bristled at my cryptic evaluation. "Listen, Rookie. The whole world system is freaking out. Finding faith in a freaked-out world is our only way to be fully alive, fully human, and fully free. Stop talking, focus on the wounded people in front of you, and work the process."

That was the only time I ever heard Art raise his voice. Normally he spoke in the soft, intelligent tones of an untroubled librarian. His point, however, was clear and unforgettable.

I focused on the doctor in front of me and imagined her as one of the courageous biblical midwives who, in defiance of the death threats of the powerful Egyptian Pharaoh, delivered their own deliverer in the infant Moses.[2] Had they not stood firm in their true identity as daughters of the Most High God, they would have perished in the false identities of victimhood and slavery.

"Take a deep breath and relax," I told her. "You don't have to fight against everything in your life. You think you're not as smart as your coworkers and that you have no real value. That's not true. Listen to God's voice, the voice of absolute truth and unconditional love. Receive. What identity does the voice of love call you?"

Eyes closed, she began to rock back and forth gently. A single tear ran along the contour of her face and fell into her rising hand.

"Oh my," she whispered. "Love calls me a healer to the nations. I need to go to the nations."

Within a year, she and her family relocated to another country in order to work with marginalized people. If you ask her today who told her to go, she will tell you it was the Holy Spirit. She realized that she had been hearing that voice her entire life; she just didn't know who it was. Now she does. Now she listens and everything is different.

This book is dedicated to the midwives of the world and Art (nmn) Blumfield and anyone else who, like the apostle Paul, thinks it's a good idea to move past all the garbage the world is offering us and into the fully alive, fully human, fully free Holy Spirit life offered to us in our relationship with Christ, who is the way, the truth, and the life. In him, we really can find transformational faith in a freaked-out world.

Acknowledgments

I wish to thank Pastor Dave Nelson at K2 the Church in Murray, Utah, for initiating and hosting the men's retreat where these ideas were given voice.

I wish to thank Josh Metcalf, who heard a recording of these words and challenged me to put them in written form.

And I wish to thank Vicki Crumpton of the Baker Publishing Group, who read these words and challenged me to write them well.

ABIDING

Once upon a time, a king came to earth to tell stories,
and the stories contained the mystery of eternal life.

JARED C. WILSON

Jesus told them a story to teach them that they
should keep on talking with God and not give up.

LUKE 18:1 WE

With many stories like these, he presented his message to
them, fitting the stories to their experience and maturity. He was
never without a story when he spoke. When he was alone with
his disciples, he went over everything, sorting out the tangles,
untying the knots.

MARK 4:33–34 MSG

On a sweltering July night in 1983, I paced anxiously in the
parking lot of the police substation, waiting to meet the field
training officer who would own my life for the next twelve

months and determine my vocational future. The scuttlebutt among the four other nervous new recruits pacing the parking lot that steamy night was "whichever FTO you get, pray to God it's not the Troll."

The Troll, as he was unaffectionately known by all police rookies, was one of the most feared training officers in the police department. If the rumors were true, what the Troll lacked in interpersonal skills and human kindness he made up for in making the life of a new recruit a nightmare and smirking proudly as the beleaguered rookies turned in their gun and badge and sought employment somewhere else—anywhere else.

All of us froze and held our collective breath as the five FTOs exited the building and began examining a list to determine which rookie was "theirs." I had neither seen nor met the Troll before, but he was easy to identify among the other FTOs. Much shorter and wider than his fellow training officers, the Troll didn't bother to consult the list. Instead, he eyed our huddled group—and we were actually huddling at this point—and yelled out across the parking lot: "Which one of you [series of expletives] rookies do I get to fire? Let's just end the [series of expletives] misery tonight and save time."

With the sweat pouring out beneath my bulletproof vest, I began praying, probably as intensely as I have ever prayed in my life, "Please, Jesus, do not let the Troll be my FTO. Please. I'm sorry for every sin of commission or omission in my life. Please give me anyone other than the Troll."

Then, as if prophetic, the Troll called out in a raspy, decidedly malevolent voice: "Is anyone over there praying that I won't be your FTO? If you are, guess what happens?"

Oh no, I thought, *a spiritual catch-22.*

In horror, I watched as the other FTOs joined up with their rookies, climbed into their respective police cruisers, and drove away. The remaining FTO approached as I stood alone and unprotected a mere few feet away from the infamous, florid-faced, fouler of fortunes and futures—the Troll himself.

God help me.

"Are you university educated, Rookie?" the Troll asked, leaning in closer. His breath smelled of kielbasa, onions, and just a hint of whiskey. Although I was a foot taller than the Troll, I felt dwarfed by his persona.

"Yes, sir."

"So, you're smart?"

I knew better than to answer that question.

"I didn't go to college. Are you smarter than me?"

Again, I employed the wisdom of silence. Plus, I was too intimidated to speak.

"Nothing to say, huh?" The Troll circled me slowly, clicking his tongue in disgust, like a farmer examining a weevil-decimated cornstalk. When he completed his inspection and we were face-to-face once again, he continued his less than inspiring introductory remarks. "I've got one simple rule for you, Rookie. For the time you and I will be abiding together, you are not allowed to talk at all unless I give you permission, and that will be seldom. Do you understand that?"

I nodded my head but I was thinking, *Did the Troll just use the word* abiding? *Did this great nemesis of the neophyte cop employ the word* abiding *because he was a fan of the Bible or* The Big Lebowski?[1]

"The reason you will not be talking," the Troll continued, "is because when you are talking, I am not talking. And when I am not talking, you are not listening. And if you are not listening, then you are not learning. So your goal for the next year, if you remain with me that long, is to keep your mouth shut, listen, and learn. If you can do that, you might live through this. Got it?"

I nodded my head again but I was thinking, *Did I just hear a really good sermon on prayer?*[2]

"Say you get it," the Troll shouted.

"I get it, sir."

"Then get in the [expletive]³ cruiser, and let's get started. You drive; I'll talk."

In the year that followed, I spent fifty weeks of four-day, ten-hour shifts with the first real discipler of my life. Although the Troll was not a Christ follower, he understood the art of discipleship better than anyone I had met previously.

The first question the Troll would ask me at the beginning of a shift was, "Are you sure you want to stay with me?"

I always felt as if this was the question Jesus himself would have asked me if he were my field training officer. "Are you going to stay, remain, dwell, continue, abide in and with me today?"⁴

With this comparison in mind, consider the types of questions the Troll asked me in some form or fashion during almost every shift. I've categorized them for convenience's sake.

Vocational

Are you ready to listen and learn from me? Do you understand that without my guidance you will not be a good cop and you will be terminated? Do you understand that if you stay with me through the year, you can become a highly productive and effective police officer? Why are you trying to be a police officer? Are you trying to be macho? Are you trying to prove something to somebody? Wouldn't you be better at some other job? Are you afraid of me? This job? Failure?

Tactical

Why did you just do what you did? Do you think about what you're going to do before you do it? Ever? Why did you say those particular words to that person? Do you think about what you're going to say before you say it? Ever? Are you afraid to think?

Marital

How is your marriage? Do you have sex with your wife every day, month, or year? Does your wife like you being a cop? What are you going to do if you're offered sex on the job? Will you tell your wife? How truthful are you with your wife? Are you afraid to communicate with your wife?

Personal

Do you know who you are? Who are you? Are you a racist? Are you sexist? Do you have a problem with poor people? Do you have a problem with rich people? Do you have a problem with homeless people? Do you have a problem with people from other countries? Are you willing to die for people you don't like? Are you willing to die for people who don't like you? Are you afraid to die?

If I failed to give a truthful, transparent answer according to the Troll's liking, he would shout, "Stop it, Rookie. Try again."

After one of these invasive interrogations, the Troll typically launched into some bawdy, Chaucer-like police parable, most of which are unrepeatable, to help illustrate or drive home his main teaching point, which was usually something along the lines of "Oh, unteachable and unresponsive rookie, how long must I tarry here with you?"

Imagine ten hours a day of these types of questions and subsequent stories. And yet, can you not see, at a much more redemptive and encouraging level, Jesus teaching in this same manner? Jesus didn't preach formulaic, chapter-and-verse sermons to his followers. He didn't lead them through a linear outline of propositional truth points. He spent time with his disciples, asking a lot of questions and telling a lot of stories—stories that we are still trying to understand today. Matthew describes a day with Jesus: "All Jesus did that day was tell stories—a long storytelling afternoon" (Matt. 13:34 MSG). And Jesus not only walked his followers into lives of truth, he was truth itself.

Like Jesus with his disciples, the Troll was not asking me these probing questions while sitting in a classroom or a men's group at a coffee shop or at a couple's retreat in the woods. He was challenging me in real time, in real-life scenarios, where people, including myself, were often in their worst and most compromising, violent, fearful, and desperate moments.

Think about it. When did Jesus hit his followers with the big questions? Wasn't it within the messiness of real-world experiences? In the heat of the argument? In the depths of fear and failure? In the face of death?

At the end of every shift, the Troll challenged me with this question: "Since I don't think you're going to make it, do you want to resign now?"

Remember the question Jesus asked his disciples in John 6:66–67? "After this, many of his disciples left. They no longer wanted to be associated with him. Then Jesus gave the Twelve their chance: 'Do you also want to leave?'" (MSG).

After every single shift, when I had left the presence of the Troll, my wife asked, "How was your shift?" My answer was often, "I don't think I'm going to make it. The Troll is making my life miserable. Why keep trying?"

Why didn't the Twelve leave Jesus? What made them stay? It wasn't as if Jesus was guaranteeing them a happy, quiet, prosperity-filled life of leisure and comfort. He was leading them straight into their deepest, darkest fears. Why did they remain?

Peter's response to Jesus's challenge is stunning: "Lord, to whom shall we go? You [alone] have the words of eternal life [you are our only hope]. We have believed and confidently trusted, and [even more] we have come to know [by personal observation and experience] that You are the Holy One of God [the Christ, the Son of the living God]" (vv. 68–69 AMP).

Peter, at least in this moment, understands that being with Jesus is not a contractual, transactional, quid pro quo that is worthwhile as long as it's working to his advantage. In fact, Peter explains his relationship with Jesus as quite the opposite. It's a divinely initiated, covenantal relationship, the benefits of which are quite one-sided. Jesus *alone* has the words of eternal life and Jesus is the *only* hope because Jesus is the *absolute* Holy One of God, the Christ, the Son of the living God. Peter's part is to receive.

How does Peter know all this? How has he come to believe and confidently trust the spoken (Greek, *rhema*) "eternal life" words of Jesus? He becomes persuaded through the process of personal observation and experience with Jesus, and this process is called abiding.

Abiding, according to Dr. John Piper,[5] is the act of receiving and trusting all that God has and is for us in Christ. Jesus tells us simply, "Abide in Me, and I in you" (John 15:4 NKJV). *The Passion* translates verse 4 as "So you must remain in life-union with me, for I remain in life-union with you."

Why did Peter refuse to leave his "association" with Jesus? Because he was not in an association with Jesus; he was not even in a mere friendship with Jesus. Peter learned through personal observation and experience that he was in life-union with Jesus and, more astoundingly, Jesus was in life-union with him. Who would want to leave life-union with Jesus?

This abiding, life-union with Jesus is available to us today and includes all the fullness of the Godhead; spiritual fruitfulness; the fullness of the words, love, and joy of the Father; answered prayer; and the glory and honor of God.[6] I ask again, who would want to leave that relationship?

The only way I was able to abide with the Troll throughout that agonizing year was by abiding in life-union with the God who still speaks—the God of Abraham, Isaac, and Jacob—revealed to us in Christ Jesus and poured out into us through the Holy Spirit. Every time the Troll asked me a probing question, God's Spirit asked the question more deeply. Every time the Troll told me a risqué story or offered an inappropriate illustration, God's Spirit beautified the story and made the illustration redemptive. Every time the Troll cursed or belittled me, God's Spirit reminded me how much he loved the Troll. And every time the Troll asked me if I wanted to quit, God's Spirit asked, "If you quit, who's going to tell the Troll I love him?"

The night that my probation ended, the Troll looked at me and said, without any sense of ceremony, "You made it. I'm cutting you loose."

I stood there staring at him, thinking of the words of Jesus on the cross: "It is finished!" (John 19:30).

"You're now allowed to talk freely," he said. He tried to smile, but it looked forced and painful and came out more as a sneer.

"Thank you, sir."

"Don't call me sir. We might become friends."

"Am I on my own now?" I asked.

"No," he snapped. "You're a real cop now. Station 5, E-squad. You have the entire PD behind you at all times."

When Jesus was ready to cut the disciples loose, he promised them as friends[7] that they would never be left alone but that the Father would send them the Holy Spirit, who would guide them in all truth and continually point them back to Christ and the things to come.[8] First John 4:13 tells us, "By this we know [with confident assurance] that we abide in Him and He in us, because He has given us His [Holy] Spirit" (AMP). In other words, if we abide in Christ, the entire kingdom of God is not only with us, it's within us.

In 1985, when I was named Police Officer of the Year, I owed my success to four persons: the Father, Son, Holy Spirit, and Master Police Officer known as the Troll, all of whom I love from the deepest part of my heart to this day.

Although the Troll has long since retired, the Trinity remains ever active and ever present. Furthermore, the Trinity is continuously inviting us into a deep, transformative life-union within the Godhead.[9] Therefore, I have a suggestion. Let's try what Peter did and personally observe and experience what happens when we abide in life-union with Christ. You see, a person doesn't *learn* to abide. A person abides and then *learns* what happens as a result of abiding. I didn't *learn* how to spend ten hours a day with the Troll; I spent ten hours a day with the Troll and *learned* the value of his training. So let's commit to spending one ten-hour shift abiding in Christ together and see what happens. OK? Great.

Here's what you need to know.

First, I am your field training officer.[10]

Second, as your FTO I have one simple rule for you, reader. As you read this book, you are only allowed to *receive* from God all that he has for you in Christ through the Holy Spirit.

Third, as your FTO I will teach through telling stories, looking at various Scripture passages, and asking questions. I, however, will not be answering the questions posed; we will be listening to God and writing down the answers he gives through his Spirit.

Fourth, as the disciples of Jesus spent time abiding with him, they became more attentive to the things of God, which led them to a greater awareness of the world around them. This awareness impressed upon them their great need to hear and understand the annunciations[11] of Jesus, which directed them into lives of transformative action. Abiding = Attention, Awareness, Annunciation, Action. In our shift together, we will walk through this process.

Finally, the narrative that follows is from an actual ten-hour (7 a.m.–5 p.m.) interaction between three hundred people and me as we spent a day together abiding with Christ. I suggest that you also set aside a day to work through the material in a single encounter and see how it impacts you. I want you to experience how much can happen in your life in just one day with Christ. Trust me, you'll want more.

Got it?

Then get a pen, a notebook, and a Bible, and let's get started. I'll ask some questions and tell some stories, and God will talk.

PART 1

ATTENTION

What is mankind that you make so much of them,
that you give them so much attention . . . ?

JOB 7:17 NIV

The best way to capture moments is to pay attention.

JOHN KABAT-ZINN

The Death of a Conversation

I walked onstage in Salt Lake City and said "Good morning" to a crowd of three hundred or so. I received a somewhat tepid "Good morning" in return.

I followed my initial greeting by asking, "How are you doing?" and received an even weaker response with a few people mumbling "good" and one person shouting out "great."

The entire interchange, based on a superficial cultural formula, was largely meaningless for most, if not all, in the room.

This often-used pattern of communication is called formulaic language formation, where I begin in a predictable manner and the audience responds in an appropriate yet predictable manner.

There are two theories of language formation: formulaic language formation and generative language formation. The first means that you use language formulas. Once you learn the language formulas, you don't have to think and create anymore. We laugh at this observation because that's what most of us do. We learn language formulas.

In the checkout line at a store, we've been taught to speak to the cashier and say, "Hey, how are you doing?" The cashier replies, "Fine, and you?" Sound familiar? This response is according to the cultural linguistic formula. It doesn't matter what they say back because I'm just going to say, "Good," pay the money, and leave. Neither of us actually cares what is really being communicated.

If you have been married a long time (I've been married thirty-six years), you can get into a formula where you know what each other is going to say. You almost don't need words. "Hey, uh, yeah." "Okay, great." That is the entire conversation because you just kind of know how it's going to go. You are conforming to worn-out language patterns.

It's not a real and dynamic relationship when you do that to people. Formulaic relationships fail, tend to flounder. Formulaic religion dies, tends to fossilize.

Jesus never speaks in language formulas. Do you know why? Because every person Jesus interacts with is a unique and distinct identity of whom he is the Creator.

Generative language formation is how Jesus talks to people. In this formation, you create a new conversation every time you talk, and it can be a lot of work. It may take awhile to get used to this style of talking as it is certainly not the American formula of communication.

Conversation in a Ride Share

One morning I called a ride share company to go to the airport. I wanted to have a conversation with the driver, so I got in the front seat when the car arrived. The driver seemed surprised, as if that wasn't the right formula for riding in a hired vehicle when you're alone.

I had lived in the Arab world for years and years, and there, you always ride in the front seat with the taxi driver. If you get behind the driver, it means you don't like him, so you always get in the front seat. And if you want him to know that you really want to talk to him, you grab his leg. But not with your left hand because that's unclean, so you have to reach across and grab his leg with your right hand.

I jumped in the front seat of the ride share, said hello, and reached over to grab the guy's leg. Startled, he jumped back against his door and said, "What are you doing?" Clearly this formula was the wrong method of communication for my Americanized driver.

"How are you doing?" I asked, attempting to recover from my mistake.

"You're going to the airport?" he replied.

"Yeah."

"Where are you going?" he asked.

"Salt Lake City."

"Do they have good restaurants there?"

"I don't know. Maybe. I don't know if people fly to Salt Lake City to eat. It's known for other stuff, not necessarily restaurants."

We were engaged in a formulaic conversation with predictable questions and responses. But these formulas reveal nothing about a person's sense of identity.

To become generative, I asked, "Besides driving folks around, what do you do?"

27

"I don't do anything except drive folks around," he said.

"Wow," I responded.

He said, "My goal is to be on vacation as much time as I can."

That's noble, isn't it? That's a noble goal. Sociologists and anthropologists say that the two highest goals of people are to be immortal and permanently joyful.

If we could, that's what we would do, isn't it? But isn't that life (immortality and joy) in the kingdom of God right now?

This guy assumed he wasn't going to be immortal, but he was going to try to be permanently happy, so he was flying to Belize as often as he could. He'd save up money and fly to Belize.

"What do you do there?" I asked.

"My goal is to open up a barbecue restaurant in Belize."

"That's interesting," I said. "Is that your identity?"

"I don't know. I guess it is."

"Running a restaurant's not an identity; it's a vocation. What is your identity? Who are you?"

"I don't know," he said. "I never really thought about that." He waited a moment, and then said, "I have a nephew who's sixteen, and he doesn't have an identity."

My driver could see the lack of identity in another person but not in himself. Isn't that interesting?

"He doesn't have an identity," he continued. "All he does is sit around and play video games. He has no sense of identity."

I asked again, "What's your identity?"

"I don't know. Where does a person get an identity?"

"Where do you think?"

"Maybe from God?" he said.

"Yes, could be," I said. "That's a possibility."

Does God talk to people? Does God talk to you? Does he say, "This is the identity I have for you"? Is that what God does? Because if God does that, that would be pretty amazing. If God talked to us and told us our identity, we would know what to do with our lives. We wouldn't have to keep going back to him and asking, "What do we do?" We would know what to do because our identity and being inform our doing.

Simple, right?

My driver wondered if identity might be God-given.

"Well, does God give identity?" I asked.

I could tell he was thinking, and I had been waiting for this. "What's your identity?" he asked.

When a person in a conversation such as this asks "What's your identity?" it's good to have an answer. Christians are good at talking about stuff that they don't ever really experience. Sometimes this can be a form of lying.

"Well, my identity is *militant peacemaker*," I said to the driver.

"Wow," he said.

"I know what vocations enable and empower that identity, and I've known this since I was fourteen. Therefore, my vocation has been with the police department, something involved in militant peacemaking."

That makes sense. I chose a vocation in the range of the identity of militant peacemaker. When I pick a vocation in that identity, I'm really, really good at it. It's easy to think this way. Conversely, if I pick a vocation outside of that identity, I'm going to be unhappy and frustrated and I'm not going to be good at it. Every day, I'm going to know I'm not good at it, and it's going to be bad. I can go to church and I can pray, but it's not going to make it better because I was not made to do whatever it is I'm doing outside of my identity.

I told the driver I was a police officer, then I got promoted a lot, then I got recruited by the government, and then I went overseas. My militant peacemaking started small and kept expanding. Professionally, spiritually, up, up, up. The gates of hell could not stand against it.

The gates of hell cannot stand against us moving in our true identity. But if we take one step outside of that identity, we're done, we're finished. It's over.

"If that's true," I said to my friend, "how dangerous is it to live a life with no sense of your identity? How dangerous?"

"You mean I would have an identity that leads to running a restaurant?" he asked.

"Yes, yes, that's it."

"And the restaurant would just be an extension of my identity?"

"Yes. That's right."

"I need to find my identity. Maybe I need to go to God and find my identity," he said.

No formulaic language in this conversation. No prefabricated gospel presentation. Just simple, generative conversation focused on this amazing young man and who he truly is to God.

This is how Jesus talks to people.

In the entire conversation, I never said one thing about being a Christian. The conversation was about personal identity, not empty ideology.

When the guy dropped me off, he asked for my card. We're going to meet so he can hear God tell him his identity. I didn't suggest that, he did. That's called sharing your faith. That's how simple it is, but you cannot give away what you don't have. You cannot give to another person something you yourself do not possess. The journey in discovering your true identity in the kingdom of God is an eternal journey. There is no end to the depths of who God made you to be.

Retreat? Never! Advance!

Recently, we did a men's identity-exchange event in a Muslim country. The men were all high-identity, high-practice Muslims. They were not Muslims who are mad at Islam or Muslims who want to change religions. The participants at this event all loved being Muslim.

It was a three-day event walking the participants through the process of understanding their true identity found only in relationship to Christ. There were some cultural nuances, but basically it is the same process you'll learn in this book.

Our main speaker was a Muslim PhD in Sharia law. The first thing he did when he stood up was to share his name and where he was from in the Muslim world.

Most of the men in the room knew who he was by his reputation as an expert in Sharia law and as a very outspoken Muslim leader. He gave his credentials, which is what you do in an Islamic context so people know who they're listening to (formulaic). He then concluded his introduction with "And my highest qualification to speak to you these three days is that I am a follower of Jesus the Messiah."

How generative is that statement? Talk about disruptive.

People started shouting.

I don't know if you've ever seen Muslims in a room when they're upset. They're not internal processors. It's all external.

Our team had been praying about doing this type of event for ten years. We'd been asking God, "How can we pull this off?"

The answer is all part of the process I'll share with you in the pages of this book.

There are brilliant ideas within you. But how do you get those ideas to live? How do you get this word, this idea in your mind, to become flesh?

Jesus is the Word of God, the idea of God rescuing humanity by becoming flesh. Jesus is the Word that comes alive and walks among us.

Everyone has ideas that need to become flesh and live outside of us. Amazing ideas, things we've dreamed about, things we don't even know we know yet but we're going to start to know.

These Muslim men were people, and like people whose worldview is threatened or challenged, these men stood and screamed, "No! We cannot accept this."

Fear shuts down creativity and the reception of new ideas.

After a few more words of introduction, the group calmed down a bit and the speaker continued: "We are going to go through the Bible together and discover, as Muslims, the true identity of the person of Christ."

Again, the room erupted in protest. We had no Christians in the audience. None. All were Muslims. I and the six American guys I had invited to help facilitate the event were all back by the exit sign, prepared to flee if necessary.

Then the speaker began to teach.

Three hours in, the participants were still screaming and yelling, and the speaker was yelling back at them, so like a good moderator I interrupted. "Okay, let's take a break. Let's calm down and take a break." *This is going to be three long days*, I thought.

One of the Muslim men became frustrated with me. "We don't want a break," he said. "We're not Americans."

Surprised, I wondered, *What does that mean? Do you think Americans just come into a seminar or class and immediately wonder when the break will be?*

Yes, I thought. *That is what we do. That's exactly what we do.* What a perceptive observation. Why is it that we often look for the quick answer, the get-spiritual-quick scheme that will magically turn us into the person we think we are supposed to be?

At 12:30, I called out, "Lunch."

Another of the Muslim participants responded, "This is our food. We must digest this important news."

They wanted to understand what the teacher was saying because he was one of their people. They identified him as "one of us." That's how important perceptions about identity are. The speaker was one of them, and he was telling them that the only way to really live this life and the life to come is through the life, death, and resurrection of Jesus.

The speaker had a very distinct strategy for how he worked his way through different, very controversial ideas.

He would first make an introductory statement such as, "According to the Al-Quran, the Bible cannot be corrupt."

Everyone would scream in opposition, but the speaker would calmly work through the evidence and methodically prove the point. At the end of the hours-long session, after they'd all calmed down and he had worked his way through the topic, he would go around the room and ask each of the thirty participants, one by one, if they now agreed with the new idea.

Seated directly in front of the speaker was the head of Islamic Studies in a public-school system. Every time he got to this guy, the room quieted. "Do you agree?" the speaker would ask. "Because we're not going forward until every one of you agree. If you don't all agree, we're doing it again."

One of the reasons the participants wanted to find agreement was because they were so moved by the powerful teaching of someone with whom they identified so deeply. He wasn't trying to convert them to another religion. He was simply leading them into identity transformation.

Believe me, these men were not the type to just say anything to make you feel good. I know, I've tried speaking in front of them.

"Do you agree?" the speaker asked each participant.

"Yes, I now agree," each responded.

In the final session, the speaker began with this statement: "We must, as Muslims, receive the gift of Jesus as our Savior. He is the only way into the kingdom. He is the only hope we have for the future."

The participants squirmed uncomfortably but still listened.

The speaker worked through the idea, and then at the end he asked each person, "Do you agree that you must receive the gift of Jesus from God? Do you agree?"

One of the participants was a journalist from a Middle Eastern magazine. We were nervous to have him in the room, but we thought, *God's not afraid, is he?* The article he later wrote, chronicling the three-day event, was beautiful. It was an article about identity transformation and peace.

The speaker finally came to the head of Islamic Studies in a public-school system. "Do you agree that we must receive the sacrifice of Jesus as the way into the kingdom? That this is the only hope for the Muslim people of the world? Do you agree?"

The room was silent. Then he looked at the speaker and said, "I've wanted to believe this my whole life; I just didn't know we were allowed to. Yes, I agree."

All the men clapped in agreement.

Afterward, some of the men came to me and wanted to know when we could organize another three-day retreat. They decided that three a year would be ideal. They also decided to invite the faculty of six Islamic schools so that their young people could be exposed to these new ways of thinking and understanding. I've already received emails from Muslims in Saudi Arabia, Egypt, and Tunisia who have been told about this event and want to come.

Praise God.

If that kind of transformation can happen in Muslims, what about in you?

Be Released! Please!

There are ideas inside your mind, heart, and spirit that no one has ever thought of before. And the beauty is that these ideas want to come out of you. The sad part is that for most of you, it's not going to happen because your false self—your fear, guilt, and shame—will shut down your creative and imaginative true self.

But there's good news! It can happen, and it can start today. You could say no to it today as well; you have that freedom. But I hope you won't. I hope you will not dare to say no to what is within you.

The world needs what you have. The world needs the real you.

I'm not talking about Christianity. I'm talking about whatever it is you know that we don't yet know. In this book, we'll dig into that. You're going to get a taste of abiding, and when you do, you're going to want to be in a community where you're doing this with others every week.

I'm involved in a small group, not a handpicked group but a random group of people from the church my wife and I attend. The group comprises four couples and three single people. We focus on listening to God and living in true identity.

From our weekly gathering, four new enterprises have emerged. One of the women in the group started a refugee-care program, and it has become one of the best refugee-care programs in the country. I invited this twenty-eight-year-old young woman to join me at a conference in Detroit, which has one of the largest refugee centers in the United States. She spoke about her strategy, and in the audience were people representing President Obama, who was in office at the time. The "experts" stared at her and asked, "Where have you been? How did you accomplish this?" They wanted to know how she had gained this expertise in refugee care and asked her to speak at their main forum in Houston.

All this from understanding true identity.

You know when that idea came to her? "It's been a pattern since I was five years old, of being a caregiver," she told me. Five years old. You know when she decided to act upon the idea? When she was twenty-seven years old. That's how long the idea had been inside her. She couldn't access it apart from God. It was there, waiting to be discovered.

One of the men in our group shared an idea about opening a fitness center for marginalized communities in our city. It's a brilliant idea.

"How did you come up with that idea?" I asked.

He said, "I've kind of just known to do it."

"How long have you known?"

"Ten years."

Ten years. The idea had been buried down inside of him in fear, guilt, and shame within a deep sense of unworthiness and inadequacy. The idea could not be realized because he didn't know his identity. He didn't know how to give birth to the idea. But the Bible narrative is all about creativity bursting forth from the true self, the true you.

Let me share my creative process within my true identity and how I prepare for an event.

When an event is scheduled, I spend a lot of time with the Lord. Because people are unique individuals, any kind of canned, formulaic talk is a waste of time. I refuse to share formulaic presentations with people. If I were you and I paid money to come to an event and heard a canned presentation, I would leave.

When I'm preparing, I ask the Lord, "What do you want to do with this group? There are people in this group you want to talk to."

I arrive at the venue and meet with the organizers and volunteer team, and we pray together. Then I go back to the hotel and work out. This is just my process to get my mind lined up with the Spirit.

While I'm working out, I'm asking the Lord to let me focus on him and what he has to say to me about this gathering—for example, the one in Salt Lake City. "What do you want me to know and what do you want me to do in relation to the men there? Is there any part of me that is not in line with hearing your voice and acting from my true identity found in you?"

For this particular event, while working out I think of the book of Hebrews. The book of Hebrews talks about rest, different kinds of rest. There's spiritual rest and geographic rest and domestic rest, but Hebrews is about rest in relation to being fit.

My fitness buddy says, "There's a sickness, wellness, fitness continuum." If you're familiar with CrossFit, you might know this. "There's sick, and then there's well, and then there's fit. Well people when they feel bad, they get sick. Fit people when they feel bad, they get well."

We want to be mentally, physically, and spiritually fit.

We don't want to be well; we want to be fit.

Your mind, body, and spirit are one in relationship, just like the Father, Son, and Holy Spirit. Your mind, body, and spirit work in relation to one another. If one part is unfit, they all struggle. It's a fact.

After working out for an hour, I return to my room and read, read, read, read. Whatever comes to my mind, I read it.

"Why am I reading this, Lord?" I ask, writing notes to myself. "What does this have to do with these men?" But I know God's going to put it all together. This process might sound strange, but I love how God does this with me.

In this journey, you will learn the process of how God speaks to you, and you're going to love walking through the process.

I read from a variety of different items, and then that's it. I'm done. I set my alarm, close my eyes, and fall asleep.

At 1:50 a.m., I wake up. "Ah! I know. Now I get why I was reading that."

Some of my friends who have worked with us, especially ones who are engineers, tell me that when they are wrestling with a particular problem, they will hold a pen in their hand and try to get to a place where they're very relaxed but not quite asleep. If they fall asleep, the pen they are holding will drop and wake them up. They want to get to that place between wakefulness and sleep where their rational mind can expand outward. In this mental state they're able to stop thinking of all the reasons why a particular problem *can't* be solved.

That's how we think. We have a dream and then wake up. But once awake, we dismiss the dream or idea, often focusing on why the dream will never become a reality.

These engineers are trying to get to the conceptual place where the *it can't happen* doesn't enter their mind. In this intuitive conceptual mental state, they can view a particular problem in innovative ways and search for solutions outside of restrictive rational thought.

This intuitive state is also called prayer or meditation. We see it in the Bible in all the beautiful passages related to prayer and meditation. It's not magic. Your mind/brain is designed to transcend the rational. That's what it does; that's what it longs to do.

The enemy's goal is to limit and narrow our thinking so that we can't see anything new but continue to tell ourselves why things cannot or will not work. We have an enemy who daily says to us, *Here's why that's not going to work.* Plenty of other people will tell us the same thing.

When we pray, God tells us how things do work, and we need to be able to hear him above the voices that tell us how things don't. Prayer is this place, up and out of ourselves, where nothing is impossible.

I'm awake from 1:50 a.m. until maybe 3:00 a.m., a flow of ideas racing through my mind—speak like this, share these ideas with them, use these examples.

All for the people at this particular event in Salt Lake City.

When our time together is done, those ideas and processes in my mind will be gone. I don't write them down because I don't want to ever do another presentation in exactly this way. That's generative language theory. It's how Jesus talks to us all the time.

God never comes to you in a formula, and he never will. You know why? He respects and loves you too much to talk to you that way. He's creative in how he talks. He's mysterious.

Three Great Mysteries

If you're ever bored, know that it's just because you're not thinking. You do understand that, right? I have three sons. Whenever they said, "We're bored," I'd say, "There's the broom. It's for bored people, and there's lots of stuff to sweep. You'll find that while you're sweeping, there are a million things to think about."

Don't sit there doing nothing. That doesn't cause your mind to transcend; it dulls your mind instead. It makes you less fit. Get the broom and start sweeping. When you do, your mind will relax, and the intuitive parts of your mind—the dream parts, the creative parts—will start running wild.

In our lives, there are three great mysteries to explore every day:

1. *The mystery of God and his universe.* Every day we can explore the mystery of the universe. All humans love to look up at the sky. By wondering about the sky, humans have figured out planetary motion and gravitational force; they have discovered other planets and how to possibly travel there. The ones who have committed their lives to understanding this mystery have said, "We're going to figure it out even if we die trying." And when they figure out one thing, they learn there's much more to know.

   Each day, try to understand more of the mystery of God and his universe: "God, teach me something about you and your universe that I do not know." You'll be doing that into eternity. He will reveal aspects of himself you never knew.

2. *The mystery of you.* Trust me, you do not know yourself. If you did, you would be doing amazing things.
   The way you think of yourself is way too small. The
   way we think of the universe is way too small. Each
   day, try to understand more of the mystery of you:
   "God, teach me something about myself that I do not
   know." In Psalm 139, David says, in so many words,
   "God, search me and know me, and reveal any wicked
   or offensive way in me, and then lead me in a new way.
   Lead me in the way of everlasting every day" (see vv.
   23–24 AMP). What hinders you from living like this?

   Once the false self is gone, you are free to become
   more than you can ask or imagine.

3. *The mystery of others.* Consider the mystery of other
   people in your world—your kids, spouse, neighbors.
   Try to figure them out. After thirty-six years, I'm still
   working on the mystery of my wife. I've known her
   since she was nineteen, and she's a beautiful mystery to
   me. My children are each a beautiful though sometimes
   troubling mystery to me. I love the journey with them,
   and with Muslims and my neighbors and many others.
   Each day, try to understand more of the mystery of others: "God, teach me something about someone else that
   I do not know."

Here's the problem for most people: in the false self, we don't
care about the universe or others, which means we don't care
about ourselves.

Ask the Lord each day, "Teach me something about another person on my street." Remember what I told you about
Muslims in the Middle East? What do we really know about
other ethnic or religious groups? There are sixty-nine worldwide movements of Muslims coming to Christ. A movement
is defined as being more than two thousand in number with

at least one thousand baptisms, three generations wide, one hundred new churches, and totally voluntary.[1] There are ISIS members coming to faith in Jesus and leaving their lives of violence and substance abuse. Christians are sacrificing their lives to reach out to and love militant Muslims around the world.

Within the exploration of these three beautiful mysteries, Jesus says our core motivation must be absolute love. Love allows us to receive without fear. Perfect love casts out all fear.

Try to love God with all your heart, all your mind, all your soul, and all your strength—your entire body, every part of you. What a challenge.

If you endeavor to love God with your mind, your mind is opened up beyond the rational into the intuitive. The intuitive mind is the place where we pray and dream and hope for things as they ought to be, things yet unseen by the rational mind.

If you endeavor to love God with your heart, you engage the emotional intelligence center of your being. Both negative and positive emotions become invitations from God into transformation.

If you endeavor to love God with your soul, life becomes nearly unimaginable—the impossible moves into the sphere of possibility.

If you endeavor to love God with your body, you will physically change. You will look different. You will move beyond being well into being fit.

Engage the three mysteries every day. The Hebrew prophet Isaiah gives us a picture of this engagement and transformation process when he writes about looking up to God, then into the self, and then outward to the other.[2] It's an amazing process that moves us from the false into the true and moves us to meaningful action in our true identity.

The way for things to be unlocked in you and in your spirit is for you to pay attention. Pay attention to God. Pay attention to things in this world. We are so distracted that we are not paying attention to what's really happening.

A Doctor and His Dog

In the late '70s when I was an undergrad at university, I had a professor, Nick Pappas, a PhD in political philosophy.[3] He was one of the best professors I've ever had in my life. He was crazy and also famous for a book about Vietnam.

Dr. Pappas was an All-American linebacker for the University of West Virginia and drafted by the Pittsburgh Steelers. He turned down the position with the Steelers to enlist in the Marines and serve his country in Vietnam as a platoon leader. He enlisted because he grew up sitting in a barber shop and listening to his father, grandfather, and uncles talk about the great wars and being a defender of freedom.

In Vietnam, he was running through the jungle and stepped on a land mine that blew up the right side of his body. Half of his right ear was gone, and he walked with a limp. A real big guy who still wore a Marine high and tight haircut, Dr. Pappas often paced back and forth in front of the class with his decided limp. Though he couldn't hear out of his right ear, he could have had the ear itself repaired, but he liked the way it looked. If you asked him a question from his right side, he would turn abruptly and ask you to repeat the question.

There were no military representatives or recruiters allowed on the university campus in those years. At that time, being a Vietnam vet was considered shameful by peace activists, but Dr. Pappas never let anyone rob him of his true identity. Despite his clear military bearing and stories of heroism and horror in Southeast Asia, students adored him.

He loved getting students riled up about political philosophy. He was so unpredictable (generative) in class that students lined up to take any course he taught. You had to get on a waiting list to get in his classes because he was an amazing, creative teacher. He was a giant and humble genius, and he knew how to get students to pay attention.

One method Dr. Pappas used to hold the attention of his students was to talk to his imaginary dog, Ranger. Students never knew when Dr. Pappas would suddenly start shouting commands to Ranger.

Once, a student asked Dr. Pappas if he could actually see Ranger.

"Of course I can see my dog," he said, laughing.

"Then why can't I see Ranger?" the student pressed.

"Because you're not paying attention to where Ranger really is in the room. And you're not paying attention because he's not your dog." Dr. Pappas thought for a moment and then asked the student, "Can you see Jesus in this classroom?"

"Of course not," the student scoffed.

"That's because you're not paying attention to where Jesus actually is in this classroom. And you're not paying attention because Jesus is not your Lord . . . yet."

One day, Dr. Pappas was lecturing on Thomas Hobbes's work *Leviathan*, which is a dense, seven-hundred-page tome and one of the most influential philosophical texts produced during the seventeenth century. In the midst of his pacing, a student interrupted him to challenge some point he was making. The interruption was quite rude and disrespectful. The student launched into a tirade about the absurdity of Hobbes's view of human nature and God.

"Ranger, come!" Dr. Pappas shouted.

The student went silent.

Dr. Pappas returned his attention to the student. "How many times have you read *Leviathan*?"

"I've read it one and a half times."

"You've read *Leviathan* one and a half times?" Dr. Pappas repeated. "Ranger, heel."

"Yes," said the student, confused but quite proud.

"You should be hesitant to speak so authoritatively about a time-tested masterpiece without reading and meditating on the text at least ten times. I have read *Leviathan* twenty-five times. Ranger, hey, sit. I've read *Leviathan* twenty-five times, and I'm hesitant to quote it with the aplomb you do with one and a half times. When you've read it five times, talk to me about *Leviathan*. Ranger, come." Then he started pacing back and forth across the room again.

"Ranger, stay!" Dr. Pappas continued, "Let me tell you. If you want to read something that's supremely profound, read the Gospel of John, chapter three, verses 16–17."

He said this from the front of a room packed with students in a very liberal, antireligion university.

"How many of you have read John 3:16–17?"

A few students raised their hands.

"If anyone in this room can explain to me the wonder of John 3:16–17, just those two verses, if you get what John 3:16–17 means, please explain it to me. Because I am in wonder of those truths more than *Leviathan*, more than any work I've ever read. Read John 3:16–17 ten times, meditate upon its meaning, and come talk to me about that. Ranger, come!"

With that, he left the room. Talk about a generative, disruptive, attention-grabbing speech.

Many students, including myself, were drawn to Jesus through the amazing identity of Dr. Pappas.

Are you amazed at John 3:16–17? These statements rocked the expert teacher Nicodemus to the core.

Let's look at John 3:16: "For God so loved the world that he gave his one and only Son, that whoever believes in him shall not perish but have eternal life" (NIV). God so loves the entire world—everyone, every single one. He loves you so much that his motivation for everything he's going to do in and through your life is always and only one thing: love. God is not mad at you. He doesn't want you to feel guilty. He doesn't want you to feel ashamed. He doesn't want you to be afraid.

He wants you to be with him, Emmanuel, God with us. He loves you so much that he decided to make that happen. He had an eternal idea, and he made that eternal idea flesh. For God so loved the world that he gave—nobody took it from him, nobody earned it from him, he gave. He gave his only Son for whoever, whoever, whoever, Muslim, Buddhist, atheist, whoever believes—and here's the complicated process of receiving what God has done: you must believe.

That's it. Believe. Receive.

The only danger at the end of the day is that you don't believe.

For God so loved the world that he gave his only Son that whoever believes in him shall not die. You shall not die, but you will have life eternal, starting now, onward. Starting now, not when you're dead. Does that make sense? After you're dead, you will have eternal . . . no. Eternal life begins the moment you believe. How does that happen? That's what we'll discover together.

Let's look at John 3:17: "For God did not send his Son into the world to condemn the world, but to save [rescue] the world through him" (NIV). Where do we get the idea that God is about condemnation? Through his Son, God rescued the world. God rescued you. Rescued you from what? From fear, guilt, and shame. When? Right now. Why? In order that you can live out everything he made you to be, in community, beginning today.

How do we do that?

Pay attention. Look in the mirror and tell the truth about what is happening around you, to you, and in you. Tell the truth. In order to learn how God is getting your attention, tell the truth.

A Thousand and One Taliban

I have a friend. I've met him two times. I call him a friend because I want to be his friend.

He's an American who has lived among the Taliban for years, though I doubt you've ever heard of him or read his books. I'm certain you've never seen advertisements about his seminars because that's not what he wants. He wants the Taliban to come to faith. This American guy is like Lawrence of Arabia. He leads a group of Taliban followers of Jesus, baptized men numbering in the thousands. Do you ever hear about that on the news?

When I finally had the chance to meet this incredible man I had been hearing about for years, I looked at him and thought, *You're the guy?*

He didn't look or act like John Rambo or William Wallace or Maximus Decimus Meridius. He is a humble, soft-spoken gentleman.

I asked him about his success in his work among the Taliban, and he said it centered on paying attention to and being aware of God's love and concern for the people of Afghanistan.

No magic formula or slick presentations.

When you pay attention to God, it means you're living and speaking the truth. This leads organically into a deeper awareness of God, yourself, and others—the three mysteries. Do you see how these concepts flow together?

If you're aware, then you know what's happening around you. If you're aware of God, God makes annunciations to you. He communicates with you personally. If you are paying attention to what's going on, you will hear him speak.

Pay attention, be aware, listen for the annunciations. When God starts to talk to you, you will know how to act. You will know what to do, uniquely, in your life. You will start doing things gradually, testing what you sense from God. Resist the fear and the doubt, and you will look back in a month, then a year, and say, "This life is amazing!"

Attention, awareness, annunciation, action. These are what we'll be doing.

Let's begin paying attention to God by praying together. Don't be afraid. Don't be nervous. I'll lead, and together we will ask God to make us attentive to him.

By the end of this book, you're going to come away with some kind of action. I don't know what your action will be, but you'll know by then. For now, however, let's begin by practicing this little thing called telling the truth. In Scripture, truth telling is called *confession*.

Don't be nervous by these perceived "church" words. The word *confession* just means to tell the truth.

Confession Doesn't Mean Saying You're Sorry

I was a police officer for several years back in the 1980s. When I arrested somebody, I would bring them in and ask for a confession. I didn't ask them for an apology. We teach confession as though it were just saying, "I'm sorry, I'm sorry, I'm sorry." If a police officer hands you a pen and paper and says "Write the truth about what happened," and you write "I'm sorry, I'm sorry, I'm sorry," it resolves nothing.

We grew up thinking confession was just telling everyone and God that we're sorry about stuff. But "I'm sorry" doesn't lead to transformation.

Confession is telling God the truth about what you really believe about him, yourself, and others. It's the greatest act, a sacrament. God loves honest confession. Confession is the beginning of genuine transformation. If you don't tell God your truth, how can he enlighten your reality with his truth?

If I say to God, "I think you let me down every day, and I'm afraid to take a new job because I'm afraid you won't show up," he will always work with that. Always.

He will respond to truth. Jesus says, "For if you embrace the truth, it will release true freedom into your lives" (John 8:32 TPT). Truth always sets you free. Hiding the truth always makes you a slave. If you will not tell the truth, you're in bondage to the lie, the deception, and the rationalization. Don't apologize for your perceived reality; tell the truth about it. That's confession. Remorse is not repentance.

Confession activates repentance. Repentance is changing the way you think, turning and going a new way. God tells you the truth about who he really is, who you really are, and who your neighbor really is. God's truth empowers you to believe in a new way, which leads to thinking in a new way, which leads to acting in a new way. This is transformation.

Confession, repentance, transformation.

We practice confession and repentance all the time. Every time I feel intimidated by a situation, I say, "God, let me tell you how I feel right now." God already knows how I feel and what I really believe. I'm not faking him out. I just say, "Lord, I feel really intimidated. I feel fearful right now. I feel powerless with this person. That's how I feel." That's confession. Notice I'm not saying, "Lord, I'm so sorry for feeling afraid; please take the fear away." God doesn't want to remove the fear; he wants to transform it.

Acknowledging the truth about your fear opens the way for repentance and for your truth (fear) to be transformed by God's truth. Then you have authority over the fear rather than the fear controlling you. That is called freedom.

Several years ago, a woman friend of mine called to tell me that her husband of ten years had suddenly begun staying out late at night, spending time in a local bar drinking. She questioned him about his abrupt, very-out-of-character behavior to which he responded with shrugs and silence.

After several requests, the husband agreed to meet with me. Rather than questioning him about his behavior, I asked him to simply tell God the truth about why he was resisting going home after work.

"I'm afraid that my wife is going to leave me, so I'm preparing myself for the rejection," was his confession. "When I was young, my dad was a construction worker and my mom was a school secretary. My mom worked hard in night school and earned a master's degree in education. The week after her graduation, she abandoned the family to pursue a new life with more 'educated' people. My fear is that my wife, who is about to finish her graduate degree, is going to leave me behind because I'm just a high school–educated construction worker like my dad."

The husband literally shook with fear at the prospect of losing the woman he loved. His wife had no intention of leaving him, but his fear was driving him to bring about the separation himself. His fear also prevented him from sharing with his wife his deep sense of unworthiness.

It wasn't until he confessed his wrong belief about himself and his wife to God that he was able to hear God call him an "honorable and worthy son." Then, as an honorable and worthy son, he had the courage to confess his fears to his wife and turn and go a new direction. They laughed and cried together as God's truth brought them into deeper intimacy and understanding with one another.

God's response to true confession is always grace and mercy. He might whisper, "Beautiful. Let's work with that. No one has authority over you. No one ever has or ever will. I brought you into this situation because this is what I want to accomplish with you. This person needs you. They're hurt. They need you." Boom! Repent—change the way you think—turn around and go the new way. That's confession and repentance.

When you live in continuous confession and repentance, your life is transformed in every area: professionally, spiritually, physically. In every way, you begin to ascend.

As I guide you in asking God questions, be prepared to write. Write ideas on your phone, on paper, on your hand . . . write down what comes to your mind. You want the false things you're believing to come into the light. Don't live your life in secret. The fingerprint of Satan on your life is secrecy and shame. Writing down thoughts and impressions gets them out of your mind and into the light.

It's even more freeing to say these beliefs out loud to others you trust who are in the process with you. This is a great way to get to know one another in a small group and a much better way than using superficial formulaic introductions.

Confessing to one another is the greatest way to form true community because it draws people together. They never forget one another because they've been with each other in their fear. And they've worked through their fear into victory. Confession makes communities function together well. This is true, spiritual relationship reality.

The reason I love working with the people I do is because we confess (truth tell) to one another all the time. If you're in the military or the police or any team situation, you know that when the heat is on, everyone tells the truth. If you're afraid, you say, "I'm freaking out right now!" But even if you don't say it, everyone knows.

Silencing the Room

As a cop, I learned that when I go into a very tense situation and silence the demonic, the situation calms down. I call this exercise "silencing the room." It got to be pretty fun when I was training rookies. I would tell them, "Watch this." Then I would pray out loud and the entire room would go silent. The surprised rookie would ask, "Where did you learn that? It's not in the academy."

When you picked up this book, you brought all kinds of false beliefs with you. You can't help it; you're human. Anxiety, fear, guilt, shame—all the garbage came with you, and the enemy is attached to it. The enemy has no authority over you. But if you think he does, in that way he does. That's sort of his game. He asks you to give him permission to run your life, and you say yes by believing his deceptions: "I'm not good enough," "Nothing will ever change," "I'm stuck in this situation," "God will never use me," "I'm alone in this mess," and so on. The enemy is ruling your life, and you become what you believe.

So we're going to silence the room. We're going to silence the negative voices that disrupt our lives. Doing so puts the room and everything in it back in its rightful order. As we silence the room, your mind is going to open. As your mind begins to unlock, start writing down the ideas, thoughts, or impressions that come to you.

After praying, I'm going to ask God a couple of questions on your behalf, and I want you to write down the very first thing that comes to mind.

Pray along with me.

Father, thank you for this reader. I bless them in the name of the Father, Son, and Holy Spirit.

Father, thank you for your beloved son or daughter. We come before you, Lord God, the High King of heaven, in the name of Jesus.

Father, thank you that your beloved son or daughter was knit together in their mother's womb by you, no matter what they believe. It doesn't matter what any of us believe; the reality is that you knit us together in our mother's womb. And when you did so, you gave us an identity. You built an identity into our DNA, and your goal for us, your joy for us is that we understand that identity and live it out, and that in living it out, we become one with you. Living out our identity, we become immortal and eternally joyful. That's what happens.

This is the goal. This has been your plan from the beginning, but we've lost sight of it. We've lost track of it. So,

Lord, we come to you as family in this community, and this is what I confess on their behalf: I confess that Jesus Christ came in the flesh, that he's the incarnate one come in the flesh. As much as we understand what that means, this is what I believe. Jesus Christ came in the flesh and walked the earth, and when he walked the earth, he came to do two things. He came to destroy the works of the enemy and to make people well.

This is why Jesus came, to destroy the works of the enemy and to make people well. Lord, he taught these things as he walked around, and he taught us to know you in a different way, in a deeper way, in order to know ourselves and others. Then he was accused and he was betrayed and he was murdered by the will of God. When he died, he descended into the depths of death itself, into the place of the enemy, and he swallowed up death into his life. He rose from the dead by the power of God and in so doing rendered Satan powerless. More than that, Jesus's death and resurrection freed humanity from the bondage of the fear of death.[4] Death no longer has a hold on those who embrace Christ.

Jesus destroyed death, and he destroyed the power of the enemy. With death conquered and the enemy defeated, he came up out of the tomb because there was nothing there any longer. He came out alive, and he walked around for forty days. In those forty days, he taught his people about the most important thing—what it means to live in the kingdom of God, starting now and on into eternity. When he finished teaching, he ascended to the Father where he sits at the right hand of the throne of God in glory. There is no other name given among men whereby we must be saved, but at the name of Jesus every knee will bow. Every demon, every angel, every creature, whether there are more in the universe, we don't know, but every knee will bow.

There's no competition; there's no contest; there's nothing to be afraid of; Christ wins! Every knee will bend. Everyone will bow and confess that Jesus Christ is Lord to the glory of God. Amen.

We believe that Jesus is a high priest who was tempted in every way just like every person who exists. There's nothing I can say to Jesus that he doesn't know experientially. He was deserted, betrayed, rebuked, everything bad happened to him, and yet he did not lose his identity as beloved Son. He didn't fall short of the glory that God had for him, and his is the name above all names.

God, because of Jesus, we can come right into your presence, into the presence of the living God, right now. Because of Christ our Savior, you say to us, "Come boldly to the throne of grace in your time of need." We can come right now, especially if we're in need. Especially if there are things in our life we're afraid of, ashamed of, and feel guilty about. We come now. This is your desire, God. This is what you are longing for us. We come not by works but by grace through faith, which is a free gift. No one reading this is any better than anyone else.

Here we are, in your presence, Lord, and we ask, God, that you would silence the enemy around us in our mind and in our life. We're so used to listening to the enemy and the world and our flesh all the time. Silence the voices, we pray in the name of Jesus. We say, "The Lord rebukes you, Satan, in the name of Jesus. You have lost; you are done; you are over. We bow our knee to the lordship of Jesus Christ. We don't bow to anyone else. The Lord rebukes you, Satan, in the name of Jesus, whom you must obey."

Lord, would you fill each of us with the fullness of your Spirit? God, would you sanctify our mind and our imagination as we think about you now? You've given us the ability to dream and to imagine. What does it mean to walk into your throne room right now? It's an actual occurrence that's happening right now.

What does it mean to stand in the throne room of God? We stand above all creation with Christ.

Here we stand in your midst, Lord, and nobody talks but you. Nobody speaks but you.

Lord, fill us with the fullness of your Spirit. Silence our own voice so that our mind is tied up with your mind, our spirit bound to your Spirit, and Lord, let us begin hearing from you in a deep new way like we've never heard before or maybe even for the first time.

Lord, here's the first question we want to ask you: **God, what is the most important thing you want to say to me right now?**

In the name of Jesus, amen.

Write down the first thing you sense. Write it down right away. Don't wait. *Lord, what is the most important thing you want me to know right now?* Don't analyze it, and don't question it; just write it down. *True Lord Jesus, what is the most important thing you want me to know right now?* Don't try to figure out whether it's coming from you or God. Just write down what is in your mind or in your heart.

Lord, what is the most important thing you want me to know right now? Take time to listen and write down your first impressions—thoughts, images, or feelings.

You may not understand what you've written down, and that's okay. Many times when Jesus spoke, people didn't know what he meant. For now, practice saying out loud what you hear or see in your mind or sense in your heart. Go ahead, try it.

Perhaps you heard or sensed God saying, "Live out my gift to you. Live out the spiritual gift I have given you." When God tells you something, when you hear a beautiful affirmation like that, you need to ask yourself, Why is he saying that? Why is

God saying, "I want you to live out your spiritual gift"? Because for whatever reason, you are not living out your spiritual gift.

Perhaps you heard the Lord call you "Beloved." Wonderful! Do you know why he called you that? Because you don't truly believe he loves you. That's why he speaks to you.

People miss the significance of what God says to them. We're not paying attention to what he's saying. If he says, "Live out your spiritual gift," a good response would be, "What is preventing me from living out my spiritual gift? What do you want me to know about that?"

This exchange produces honest confession.

The Lord loves you. He will usually begin communicating to you with an affirmation and a challenge—the same way Jesus related to people in the Gospels. This is what you're supposed to be, and this is what you are supposed to do.

Maybe you heard, "Love and trust me." Good. Love and trust the Lord. Why would he say that to you? What does he want you to know?

Did you hear, "You're good enough"? Why? Could it be that you don't think you're good enough? Isn't it beautiful that God is affirming to you that he has always approved of you? It's not about works or comparison or competition. God made you enough, and that is how he has always seen you.

Maybe God said, "I love you more than you will ever know." Beautiful.

I wonder if you sensed or heard God say, "Share your faith. I have an identity for you." Sometimes God gives us action steps.

The next question is, "Lord, where in my life do I feel like I'm not beloved by you? Where in my life am I not trusting you? Where in my life do I think I'm not good enough for you? Where in my life am I listening to the wrong voice?" As you sense his response, follow up with "God, what (else) do you want me to know?" God challenges us with affirmation.

Jesus is always encouraging us: "Follow me. Come with me. Listen to me." And usually we respond with "Well, I've got all this stuff I can't carry." He says, "I know. Drop it. You were never meant to carry it."

Now that we've begun listening, we know that God does indeed love us. God is not angry with us or disappointed in us. He died for us while we were his enemies.[5]

Let's continue listening. I'm going to ask the Lord about obstacles.

> *Father, thank you for this reader. I bless them in the name of the Father, Son, and Holy Spirit.*
>
> *Father, thank you for speaking to us.*
>
> *Thank you, Lord, for your words to us, your love for us. Lord, thank you for your affirmations. Thank you that your Word is true, that God is love, and that you love us all with an unconditional love. Lord Jesus, would you continue to speak to us? Guard our minds in your Spirit. Protect us from the enemy.*
>
> *Father, here's the second thing we want to ask you:* **Lord, would you tell me or reveal to me one place in my life where I'm not living in truth?**

Write down what you sense. Don't tell the Lord; allow him to tell you. It might be different from what you think. Don't be afraid. Write it down.

> *Lord, what is one place in my life where I'm not living in truth? Search me and know me, Lord. Help me to understand myself, Lord, and show me one place in my life where I'm not walking in truth or living in truth. I want to be as honest as possible on this.*

Asking this question takes a lot of courage. Hearing from the Lord doesn't have to be a long, drawn out process. The

Lord is quick to respond when we are honest and sincere before him.

We're not looking for superficial; we don't need a long explanation. We want authenticity. We're simply asking what that one place is in our life where we're not living or dealing in truth. We're not in a counseling session; we're in a truth-telling session. That's all we're going to do. We're just going to unburden ourselves with this confession.

Write it down and then say it out loud.

The Bible says that we are to confess our sins to one another *in order that* we may be healed.[6] Wellness is connected to confessing our sins to one another. The word used for *sin* in this verse in some of the older Greek texts is *paraptōma*, meaning "a deviation from what is true." Confession is not telling all your moral failures to somebody. That's not particularly helpful. When we confess, we are telling the truth about where we have deviated or moved away from what is true about God, ourselves, and others. Moral failures are the result of this deviation.

This is different from how most of us were taught by "religion." Most of us were told that our problem is that we do wrong things. But that's not really the issue. The issue is wrong belief or believing what is not true. This wrong or false belief leads us to separate or deviate from God, ourselves, and others. The result of this separation, this sin, is wrong action.

Our tendency is to focus on wrong actions, and we miss the source, which is wrong belief.

Let's explore what others have shared they sensed from the Lord when asking the question about where they were not living in truth. Here are a few statements I've heard from my seminar attendees.

"I'm not declaring who God is to other people."

This is a statement of action, not identity, and doesn't seem like truth from God. Religion says you are a poor Christian because you do not declare God to other people the way you're supposed to or as often as you're supposed to.

My question would be, How often and to what degree are you supposed to declare God to people? What's the standard? Who sets that standard? Ask God what *he* wants you to know about that!

"I need more of a prayer life."

Another statement of action: I need to pray more. Or, conversely, I'm not praying enough. Again, how much should you be praying? Without ceasing? How often is that?

Remember the question we just asked the Lord: *Would you show me one place in my life where I'm not living in truth?*

The question is about walking and living in truth, not about doing things for God. We tend to be more works oriented, don't we?

"I'm not experiencing God in the workplace."

Wow, another action statement! This is why we can get stuck in these thoughts and never get out of them. We're not paying attention to what God is saying, and therefore we're not aware of how to pursue God into healing and reconciliation.

Imagine walking up to Jesus and saying, "Lord, show me one place in my life where I'm not living in truth."

Jesus smiles back at you and says, "You believe the lies that you are not experiencing God in the workplace because you are not praying enough and declaring God enough to other people."

As a follow-up, you might ask Jesus, "What is preventing me from experiencing God at a deep, personal level in my life?"

Here is a key question: How does it make you feel that you're not experiencing God in the workplace like you're supposed to? How does that make you feel about yourself?

"Shameful."

The obstacle to experiencing God anywhere in life is shame. Shame (feeling unworthy, not good enough) needs to be confessed. You know why? Shame is a false identity. Everything from "I look at pornography," "I eat too much," "I drink too much," "I don't do this," "I need to do that," and so on makes me feel one of three things: fear, guilt, or shame.

Fear, guilt, and shame are false identities. It won't matter how many accountability groups you go to, podcasts you listen to, or books you read. If you live in fear, you are still going to try to control things in order to cope with your anxiety. Your identity is fear.

If your identity is based in guilt, you will struggle with a negative sense of self-worth and self-esteem. Guilt leads to an identity of unworthiness.

If your identity is unworthiness, you will act like an unworthy person. It doesn't matter where you are or whom you are with. You'll still act to prove your worth and value. You'll set up all the chairs, or you'll be the first one at church every week. Why? Because you're overflowing with joy? No, because you're trying to prove that you are worthy.

Only God makes you worthy. Only God removes shame and replaces it with value. On the cross, Jesus canceled all guilt and its resulting shame. Your works cannot accomplish this. Receive the free gift of God.

The longer you succumb to the temptation of the enemy to prove your worth, the deeper the deception is reinforced. You are a slave in bondage to fear, guilt, and shame.

In the practice of this confession, what are we confessing?

God might say to me, "Jamie, the thing that's hurting you is the way you talk to your wife."

Does that mean God wants me to go to a seminar and learn how to talk to my wife? Maybe. But what is the actual source of the problem?

I ask God, "What do you want me to know about the way I talk to my wife?"

"You talk to your wife like a man who is ashamed of his past. A person ashamed of their past is defensive; their feelings are hurt easily, and they respond from woundedness."

Do you understand the role shame plays in your life?

In the garden, Adam and Eve separated themselves from God and his truth of their identity and destiny. They began deciding for themselves what is good and bad, what is right and wrong. They transferred their trust from the true life source, God, to their own knowledge of good and bad. They were trying to figure out how to make themselves good. God ceased to become their source of truth. Instead, they became their own source of truth, separate from their Creator. The irony here is that they were already good—created in God's likeness and image.

Here is life with God: "Go out and discover the mystery of the universe, yourself, and each other. Go, enjoy creation! Have fun; it's all yours. I will be with you. Stay away from that one tree, though; it'll kill you."

I think Eve eats from the tree of the knowledge of good and evil because she fears that she isn't enough.[7] She is tempted by the serpent to believe that God is withholding what she needs to be enough. Are you ever tempted to think to yourself, separate from God, and chase after things, so you feel good about who you are? You already possess deep within you everything you will ever need. Eve engaged the doubt and disconnected from her life source, then the fear crept in. The doubt produced fear. She had a choice at this point to listen to the affirming voice of God or give in to the doubt that she needed something God might not provide. She eats the fruit, and she exchanges life in all its abundance for a corrupted life: *Was that the right thing to do or the wrong thing to do? Did I say the right thing or the wrong thing? This makes me feel bad; how can I feel good again?*

The knowledge of good and evil always leads to a form of death. Always.

In accountability groups, we're asked, "Did you look at pornography?" Either we lie, say no, and feel guilty, or we tell the truth, say yes, and feel guilty. Afterward they say, "Thanks for coming, see you next week." What is that? That's Satan's accountability group.

Here's God's accountability group: "How do you have time to look at pornography if you're living out your true identity? You know why you're looking at pornography? Because you feel unworthy. You don't know your true identity, so you've lost track of what is meaningful in life. You know what your identity has become? Shame. Fear. Guilt. But these are false identities that only *feel* true."

This realization we are not living out our true identity is what God is moving us toward in times of confession.

The question we need to ask ourselves is, When did that sense of unworthiness (or fear, shame, etc.) begin?

The Spirit is leading you to the source of your sense of unworthiness. God is redeeming and reconciling your belief systems, and when they are in alignment with his love, the doubt and fear will transform into security and faith. Then your mind will begin focusing on your true identity and who it is you were always meant to be, which will then inform what you are supposed to do. Then even the mundane daily tasks will fill you with joy, and you won't have the time or desire for distracting and destructive coping mechanisms—they are just not worth it anymore. You won't have to cry out, "Help me not to do it!"

It's like there's a pile of trash down in our soul that rats are attracted to. We try to shoo away the rats, but they just keep returning. They never stop. And the things that we wish we could do, we don't do, and the things we don't want to do, we do. The rats keep coming, and we keep shooing them away.

We go to seminars and we listen to podcasts and we memorize verses, but we're still shooing away rats.

Jesus is saying, "Let me have the trash pile. I will take it." The trash pile is a belief system rooted in fear, guilt, and shame. That's all it has ever been and all it will ever be.

When you live in your true identity, nothing can stop you from the life-fulfilling destiny God has for you to discover. Let's take a look at how to get rid of that trash pile so that the rats will cease to exist.

PART 2

AWARENESS

Let us not look back in anger, nor forward
in fear, but around in awareness.

JAMES THUNDER

Satan might not outwit us.
For we are not unaware of his schemes.

2 CORINTHIANS 2:11 NIV

The Three Faces of Me: The Real, the True, and the False

When we practice truth telling, everything in our life changes, and when we start truth telling with God, our relationship with him becomes more alive. We can pay attention to him because God will only speak to us in truth. That means if we're not willing to speak in truth, he's not talking. Or rather, he is talking, but we can't hear him. Those are the ground rules.

If I want to know how to pay attention to what God is doing, how to be aware of him in my life, I have to speak and live in truth. That does not mean I'm perfect. Living in truth does not mean I am without flaw; it simply means I am in the transformation process.

There are three ways to think of the mystery of myself—the real self, the true self, and the false self. The real me isn't afraid to tell the truth as I see it. The real me is realistic about who I am: I'm really unhappy, I'm really afraid, I'm really fearful, I'm really worried. I'm saying what I believe in my heart. I'm not talking about what I know in my head. Religious people talk from the head, not from the heart: I know I'm supposed to be happy, but I'm not; I know I'm supposed to never be afraid, but I'm afraid.

In science, this heart-head connection is called neurocardiology. It's fascinating that the heart is really the information gatherer and the brain is simply the organizer and processor. The heart gathers information all the time.[1] This is why we're supposed to love the Lord our God with all of our heart, mind, soul, and strength. The heart is the receiver of the information.

The enemy does not want you to live from the heart. He wants you to live from the rational mind, because the rational mind is limited. The rational mind can create an industrial revolution, but it cannot fully understand concepts such as love, grace, and forgiveness. These ideas are transrational.

You're the Welcome Wagon?

Once while working in a Muslim country, a coworker called me from a neighboring country that was engulfed in civil strife. He informed me that the previous evening, two men began pounding on his apartment door, demanding entrance. He said, "When I looked through the peephole, I could see the men were dressed as members of an extremist militia in the area. As a newly arrived American worker in the city, I feared for the welfare of myself and my family. I pretended not to be home and the men finally left, but I'm afraid they'll come back tonight. What should I do? Should I flee the city?"

As humans, we can be quite wrong about what we think or conclusions we draw in situations where we're confident that the facts speak for themselves. This mistake occurs most often when we separate our heart from our brain and let our brain go into autopilot. In autopilot, the brain processes everything it sees in the present based on what it has seen and known in the past.

This was the case with my coworker friend. He was an experienced worker in the Middle East, but the suddenness of the event and the resulting fear hindered his ability to be attentive and aware in the new and present scenario. He defaulted into a reflexive fight-flight-or-freeze mentality.

While we talked together, he was able to silence the threatening voices of the enemy and focus his heart and mind on asking God what he wanted him to know and do in the current situation. Rather than fight, flight, or freeze, the Holy Spirit led him into a plan of active engagement.

The next night when the men returned, pounding on the door, my friend exited his apartment, locked the door behind him, and walked quickly between them into the street. The men followed him, and once gathered in the street, my friend asked, "What can I do to be of help to you and the other people in this community?"

The men stared at him for several seconds before one of them spoke up. "We know you are new in the neighborhood, and so we came to welcome you and invite you to a dinner with our families."

Rather than fleeing the city in fear and missing an opportunity to impact the neighborhood for Christ, my friend was able to turn his heart to the Father and experience the Father's heart for these Muslim men.

The heart sees each thing anew all the time. However, the brain says, "Nope, we've seen this before. We got hurt. We're not doing it again." As a result, when God says, "Hey, I have a thing I want you to do in your life; it's going to be incredible," the typical response from our rational mind is, "Nope, too risky." Think about Moses when God first called him to lead the Israelites. His response was, "Find someone else who is a better speaker." Or Gideon, whom God calls his "mighty man of valor." His response? "Nope, I'm the least in my family."

But God, in his love and patience, presses us forward. We can feel it down in our heart as we sense, "Let's do this new thing!" Then we dream and have an idea and think, "I can do this!"

And then, in our mind we say, "No. No." Why? "Because I'm not worthy. I'm filled with shame. I'm afraid. So I cannot do it."

This type of thinking hurts us. If we could live and lead with our heart, what a different life we would experience.

Once the heart and mind are brought into balance, with the mind serving the heart, we can live with an unconflicted mind. Can you imagine living with an unconflicted mind where your heart and mind are always in sync? And even greater, your heart and mind are in sync with each other *and* they're in sync with God? Imagine living like that!

I'm not talking about some religious magic world. I'm talking about real life, like on a Monday morning. I know who I am, and I know how to align my heart and mind in relationship with God. As a result, I can do anything in my true identity.

What's in a Name?

Throughout Scripture, the concept of identity or naming is very important to God. Consider Jesus's baptism at the initiation of his public ministry. "In those days Jesus came from Nazareth in Galilee and was baptized by John in the Jordan. And immediately coming up out of the water, He saw the heavens opening, and the Spirit, like a dove, descending upon Him; and a voice came from the heavens: 'You are My beloved Son; in You I am well pleased'" (Mark 1:9–11 NASB).

Jesus has always possessed this true identity, but here it is spoken publicly by God in order that the community might know and participate in it. In the same way, our true identity must be received from God within community.[2] True identity can only be known by truth telling. Truth telling moves us from what is *real* to what is *true*. This is important because what is *real* to me isn't always *true*, but what is *true* is always *real*.

I must be willing to acknowledge and confess the real me in order to understand the true me. The real me is telling the truth in any and every situation.

For example, if you ask me if I love God, speaking realistically my answer would have to be "I don't know." Do I want to love him? I think yes. But in reality, I do not know what it means to wholeheartedly love an invisible, formless, ultimate being.

I hope and long to love God; I do. That's the real me. God sees the true me whom he created. This is what I'm moving toward. I'm moving from the real me, the "God have mercy on me, a sinner," to the true me, the "you are my militant peace-maker; let's go do it together. Come with me; follow me; give me your burden and take mine. Let's go." That's the true me.

Unfortunately, where most of us live is in the false me, and the false is not even real.

I feel unworthy because I accept the false identity that I am unworthy. "I am unworthy" is an identity statement, and when I live my life according to this identity, it's painful. This is the false me.

When a person says to me, "I'm addicted to pornography," I say, "That's not who you are. You are describing an action. That's not an identity. What is your identity?" A person who is addicted to pornography has an identity that permits them to be addicted to pornography. What's that identity? Unworthy.

Unworthy people hide in secret rooms in places where they can't be rejected. Shame-filled people waste hours alone in solitude. They live in these dark, isolated places because they believe no one wants to be with them, and that feels true. It's not real, and it's definitely not true. But we interact with people as if their false identity is real and true.

Perhaps my neighbor is hostile toward me, so I return their hostility. In doing so, I verify and validate this false identity. But why does my neighbor hate me? Perhaps they're experiencing fear, guilt, and shame, which they project onto me. Then I self-protect and self-promote because my neighbor's violence makes me feel powerless and unworthy and fearful. So I project back onto them.

And here goes the conflict. The war begins.

War: What Is It Good For?

Once I was with a member of an intelligence agency in another country who told me he was frustrated. He asked me, "What would you say to defuse this situation if the leader of this terrorist organization entered this room right now and sat down?"

I said, "I would look at him and ask, 'What can we do to bless you?'"

The intelligence officer said, "That's the dumbest thing I've ever heard in my life."

"What would you say?" I asked.

"I'd tell him he's not getting anything from us."

And what's the result? War. You cannot escape it. Once you tell him he's getting nothing from you, what's the goal of his life? To get everything from you that he can. Murder becomes a logical option. What else are you going to do? Someone's got to die, right? And then you can't get out of the situation.

I asked this guy, "How long have you been at war?"

He said, "Every day of my life."

"And how long was your father at war?"

"Every day of his life."

"And how long will your child be at war?"

"Every day of their life; there's no end."

Until you stop living in a false identity, it will never change. The goal is to move from the false to the real to the true.

The Bible is a series of case studies about identity. Whatever predicament you find yourself in, look in the Bible for case studies from various cultures and from different times. Where is there a situation like yours? Right there in Babylon. Read the case study and ask, "How did that guy screw up? Oh, that's what he did."

Satan is not fearful of us memorizing verses. He quotes verses to deceive us. Likewise, Satan is not afraid of the Bible itself. We're sleeping with the Bible or waving the book at Satan and shouting, "Go away, Satan." He's not afraid of this.

What Satan fears is truth. He can't tolerate truth or truth tellers. That's how Jesus beats him every time. Jesus speaks only truth to the Liar, and the Liar can speak only deception back. Deception cannot exist in the place where truth shines.

When you speak truth, Satan moves away from you because you are submitting to God and therefore resisting the enemy. According to Scripture, this process forces the enemy to flee.[3]

Confession is the first part of truth telling.

The King and I . . . and All the Rest of Us Too

Let's look at the life of King David.

David was probably born around 1040 BC, which was during the tenth year of King Saul's reign over Israel. When David was born, his father, Jesse, was very old.[4] At around age fifteen, David had encounters with a lion and a bear, both of which he killed with a slingshot. What is that age equivalent to today? Ninth grade. As a ninth grader, David was able to shepherd his sheep and protect them from both lions and bears with his skill in battle.

From this account, we can surmise what elementary and middle school–aged David was doing with his time. He was learning to shepherd sheep, write poetry, and throw stones with a sling. In middle school or younger, David was practicing the very skills that would make him one of Israel's greatest kings.

What are our middle school–aged kids doing? Do they have an inner sense of identity that is energizing them into their future destiny? From where and from whom are our sons and daughters gaining their identity?

When young David is anointed king of Israel by the prophet Samuel, he becomes Saul's musician[5] and one of his armor bearers. There's that crazy poetry practice coming into play (pun intended).

Here's the amazing thing about this little passage of Scripture: when David is anointed king, the Hebrew Scripture says, "The Spirit of the LORD rushed upon David from that day forward" (1 Sam. 16:13 ESV). Did you catch when the Holy Spirit left David? Never.

Do you know why the Holy Spirit rushed upon him when he was anointed king? Because that was David's identity. That's the true David. The real David can kill lions and write poetry but only the true David is a shepherd-poet-warrior-king filled with the Spirit of God.

In the same way, the real you can accomplish things. But the true you can do . . . well, you don't even know. You have no idea. Whatever level you find yourself within this world, you can go higher.

This is how my own identity and destiny have been developed. Our team takes any willing person and helps them go higher. Not because we know what they should do. We just know how to know, and we teach people how to know their true identity. If true identity is knowable at a young age, why don't we know who we really are and in turn teach it to our children?

As a young boy, David is anointed into his vocation and anointed into his true identity by God. Is he a king yet? No, he's not yet officially a king. Even so, he is truly a king at this time, now and forever. The point is, David's true identity in the kingdom of God, from the day God knit him together in his mother's womb, was shepherd-poet-warrior-king.

According to the Bible, if you sense from God that you are a healer of nations and you're currently working at a gas station, you should start pursuing the skills to become someone who heals and who brings healing on a large scale. God only speaks to you in your true identity. That's the only way he'll ever talk to you. Stop coming to him in a false identity. He's not talking to a false you. He's always communicating to the unique, worthy, and loved true you. Can you hear him?

This Is Only a Test

I once prayed with a young immigrant Muslim man who worked his way through the US public school system and community college while working to care for himself and his family. When it came time to pursue his dream of attending business school, he failed the entrance test. After he failed a second time and fearing failure in his third and final attempt, he called on his Christ-following friends for prayer.

As we sat to pray with the man in his apartment, we noticed his living room wall adorned with dozens of certificates of academic achievement and praise. He was certainly capable of passing the business school entrance exam, and he told us how easily he could pass the online practice test. But when it came to the actual timed test, he was paralyzed by fear of failure.

As we led him into an experiential encounter with the living God, who had knit him together in his mother's womb, he recalled the night some men came into his village and kidnapped his father. When he awoke and found his father taken, he blamed himself for not being awake to warn him. It didn't matter that he was a very young child at the time. He felt that it was his fault, that he failed the test of protecting his father, and that he was and is a failure. When he was not under pressure, he was a very good student. But when the pressure was on, he resorted to a false identity of failure and he froze.

After confessing the false identity, he was able to listen to God's Spirit, who released him from his sense of shame and reminded him that his father did eventually return safely. "You are my beautiful student," the Lord whispered to him, enabling him to take the test in joy and peace. He is an amazing business professional, bringing hope and joy to many.

Many of us have taken on the identity of a victim. If you come to the Lord as if you are a victim—"Oh, God, I'm so unworthy. Oh, God, I'm so shameful"—his response will be something like this: "Who is this? What is that noise? All I see is my leader, my student, my beloved son, my beautiful daughter. Who is saying they're shameful? Did you say that? How dare you say that to me! I died to take away that shame. How dare you call yourself unworthy. I died to show you your value to me." The Bible tells us that God "made Him who knew no sin to be sin in our behalf, so that we might become the righteousness of God in Him" (2 Cor. 5:21 NASB). Do you get that? Because of Christ's finished work, we are to come to God as those *made* righteous.

Be aware of what God in Christ has done. Pay attention to this stunning progression of truth: "We love Him because *He first loved us*" (1 John 4:19 NKJV, emphasis added). How do we know this to be true? Because "God demonstrates his own love for us in this: While we were still sinners"—separated enemies of God—"*Christ died for us*" (Rom. 5:8 NIV, emphasis added). Why? Because "we are his workmanship"—his master work—"created in Christ Jesus for good works, which God prepared beforehand, that we should walk in them" (Eph. 2:10 ESV).

How are we walking? Like victims who blame everyone, including God, and everything else for our difficulties and failures?

Let's stand up in the true identity given to us by God and let the redeemed of the Lord say so! God talks to us only in our true identity and says, "Rise up as my leaders in a dark and fragmented world."

The Leader of the Pack

Do you know what a leader is? It is anyone who wants to see something changed for the better.

God loves leaders because every person God creates is made to be part of an eternal transformation process. As leaders are being transformed by the constant renewing of their hearts and minds, they are bringing transformation to the world around them.

This is what the prophet Isaiah said about David:

> There shall come forth a shoot from the stump of Jesse,
> and a branch from his roots shall bear fruit.
> And the Spirit of the LORD shall rest upon him,
> the Spirit of wisdom and understanding,
> the Spirit of counsel and might,
> the Spirit of knowledge and the fear of the LORD.
> (Isa. 11:1–2 ESV)

This is David. This is his true identity—shepherd-poet-warrior-king. He's a fifteen-year-old, shepherd-poet-warrior-king, one of the greatest kings who ever lived. And the God of all creation will only talk to him as his shepherd-poet-warrior-king.

How does he talk to you?

Between the ages of about seventeen to twenty-one, David fights and kills Goliath and is promised Saul's oldest daughter, Michal, whom he marries.

Around age twenty-three, David flees from Saul and befriends Jonathan. Then he flees to Nob and then to Achish, king of Gath. Then he goes to Adullam and gathers his family. There, about four hundred men come to him. First Samuel 22:2 describes them as "those who were in distress or in debt or discontented" (NIV). These are the men he attracts. What an army! Why does he attract these kinds of people? Because David knows his own identity. He's a man after God's own heart, and when these discouraged men look at David, they see the very heart of God.

David takes those four hundred people, and in about three years' time, he's leading an army of six hundred of some of the greatest warriors in Israel's history.

Who are they? Four hundred losers who are now six hundred of the very best.

How does he do that? How does a twenty-something-year-old, in that amount of time, take four hundred disenfranchised farmers, shepherds, and God only knows what else and transform them into men so skilled at warfare that they're listed by their identities and what they can do on the battlefield? They actually become known in Hebrew as the *gibborim* or the *mightiest*.

It is as if God is making a list and asking, "Who will be reading my book?" Then he starts listing the names of every individual who will ever engage with this book by the identity he calls them and what they will accomplish. Do you think God can do that? That's what God does. Because he loved the world so much, he gave his only Son so that whoever believes in him will not die but will live forever. God did not send his Son to condemn the world but so that through him the world could be rescued.

Two of the greatest of David's mighty men were renowned for their courage to stand firm when everyone else ran away. That was their skill.

I'd love to be that kind of champion. Everyone else quits. Everyone else is a victim. Everyone else goes home. Everyone else boards up their windows. Everyone else hides. But those men stood firm.

The apostle Paul encourages us in Ephesians 6:10–17 that when the enemy comes, we must stand firm. Four times the challenge shouts from the passage. Stand firm! Stand firm! Stand firm! Stand firm against the schemes of the enemy.

How do you stand firm? In the truth of who you are in the kingdom of God. The gates of hell cannot prevail against the true you.

But most of us aren't living in our true identity. We're drifting in between the false and the real.

Now You See Me, Now You Don't

In 1 Samuel 26, David and his six hundred men are up in the hills, and he's waiting. If you think about it, David is operating an illegal army inside of a kingdom that is not yet his. Saul is the king. Saul rules the country, and David is operating his own army inside that country. What would we call that person today?

Imagine a private citizen operating a fully functional army inside the United States that is not sanctioned by the government of the United States. What would we call that leader? An insurgent? A terrorist?

In this story, David learns that Saul and his leaders are camping down in the valley. Saul is asleep.

David asks his men, "Who would like to go down into the camp after Saul with me?" What does that say about David?

He's fearless. But why? There is a reason why he's fearless. He knows he's a king, though he isn't yet king. But David believes that he won't die until God completes his destiny as king.

You can't just make yourself fearless. No one in the Bible thinks, *Wow, we just have a lot of self-generated faith, so let's go do some death-defying stunts.*

People are mostly afraid all the time. In fact, the number one exhortation in Scripture is, "Do not be afraid." We can only become fearless as we follow God in our true identity and experience in real life the truth of God's promises to us.

Has David ever been in a place where he should have died and didn't prior to this event? Yes, many times. David has learned experientially not to fear death.

How do you learn not to fear death? By going into places where death is possible and experiencing God's presence. Does anyone want to do that? No. Do we really trust God at that level? Not really. We want to self-protect and self-promote away the fear, which means we can never be fearless.

David asks two of his men, "Who will go down there with me?" Only one of them answers, so apparently the other guy isn't convinced. But Abishai responds, "I'll go with you." They go down and walk through the guards. Scripture says, "They were all sound asleep, for a deep sleep from the LORD had fallen on them" (v. 12 AMP).

This story reminds me of a time when my family lived in Indonesia. The government of Indonesia collapsed. The military and the police simply disbanded, and angry mobs began looting and burning the city where we lived.

Unfortunately, or fortunately, however you look at it, we sensed from the Lord not to leave the country. Usually in these situations, foreign workers are the first ones out, which says something about our concern for the people of the country.

But the Lord said, "I want you to stay through this because I want your kids to see that I can protect them."

My wife, Donna, said, "Did he say we were included too or just the kids?"

We stayed and it was crazy. Thousands of people going up and down the streets, burning buildings and robbing people in all the big cities.

One time, we were driving down a quiet neighborhood street with our kids and some of their friends. We turned a corner and saw a mob of hundreds of people. They wore the headbands of an extremist political party. They were waving signs and sticks and broken bottles, screaming, chanting, and coming down the street, and there we were, a car full of foreigners. And I couldn't back up. Donna, suppressing the panic she felt, asked, "What should we do?"

Well, I didn't know. What do you do?

It didn't sound very spiritual, but I looked in the mirror, and said to the kids, "Pray that we are invisible right now. Pray that God makes us invisible."

And my kids did just that. They became excited, raising their hands and repeating their prayer: "God help us to be invisible, make us invisible."

As we prayed, I began to think that maybe this was a good idea after all. We didn't have sticks and broken glass, but we felt a surge of authority and power. Donna and I joined in asking God to make us invisible to the mob.

The crowd came down the street to where we were the only car in the middle of the road . . . and they went around us. They pushed against the car and shook the car, but they didn't break any windows or beat the car or try to get in the car. The crowd flowed past the car, and we swayed like we were in a flood. This lasted for maybe five minutes because the crowd was so large.

We sat in the car whispering, "Be invisible, be invisible," while the entire crowd went by. We were left unharmed and undamaged in the middle of the street.

I took a deep breath, sighed in relief, and began to drive, when my oldest son yelled out, "Dad, don't drive yet. We're still invisible. God, make us visible again." Can God still do stuff like that? Yes, he can.

Do you know how many times we've prayed that invisible prayer since that day? In many situations we've thought, *It would be good to be invisible right now.*

We can only become fearless by following God into fearful situations and experiencing his love and protection.

David and Abishai go down to Saul's camp, and Abishai says, in today's vernacular, "Oh, there he is. There's Saul right there. There's the source of all our problems." Abishai brags, "It will only take me one thrust of my spear, and he'll be dead. Just give me the kill order."

But what does David say? "Do not kill him, for who can reach out with his hand against the LORD's anointed and remain innocent? . . . As the LORD lives, the LORD certainly will strike him, or his day will come that he dies, or he will go down in battle and perish. The LORD forbid that I would reach out with my hand against the LORD's anointed!" (1 Sam. 26:9–11 NASB).

That's brave; that's faith.

And that's smart. David knows his identity. He doesn't need to manipulate things to make his identity sure. He's going to wait on God, so he holds back Abishai. Instead, they take the spear and water jug that are near Saul's head and go back up the hill. From there, David shouts down rebuke to Saul's general, Abner. "Why then have you not guarded your lord the king? For one of the people came to kill the king your lord! This thing that you have done is not good. As the LORD lives, all of you undoubtedly must die, because you did not guard your lord, the LORD's anointed. And now, see where the king's spear is and the jug of water that was at his head!" (vv. 15–16 NASB).

Saul recognizes David's voice: "Is that your voice, David my son?" (v. 17 NIV).

David responds to Saul's inquiry in the wholeness and wellness of his true identity. He humbles himself before both God and Saul and calls out, "The king of Israel has come out looking for a flea. You are like a man hunting partridges in the mountains" (v. 20 ERV).

Then Saul says this amazing thing: "I have sinned. Return, my son David, for I will not harm you again since my life was precious in your sight this day. Behold, I have played the fool and have made a very great mistake" (v. 21 NASB).

The chapter concludes with David going on his way and Saul returning home.

This is a great lesson in conflict resolution. You want to end a conflict? Let the enemy know that their life is valuable in your eyes. Love them. Doing so ends conflict. But we won't do that if we think it is a position of weakness. Yet, it is what David does, and Saul and his army walk away.

The Dis-ease of Introspection: Walking Side by Side with Myself

When David was about age twenty-seven, he made a significant mistake. He made a lot of mistakes; he was human. But in this instance, he made a really big one. It's a fascinating passage. This is perhaps why you need to look at the Bible differently than you have in the past. Don't only read the Bible in some formulaic pattern. Instead, ask God, "What does this say to me? How is this related to my identity? What do you want me to know?"

You might truth tell and confess that a certain Scripture passage frightens you. Ask the Lord, "Why am I afraid? What am I afraid of?"

After his amazingly brilliant strategy of not raising his hand against Saul and killing him but waiting for God to protect and promote him, David becomes afraid.

Why? What happens is that David, rather than "inquiring of the Lord," which is his usual and successful modus operandi, tries human introspection instead.

Scripture records the event this way: "But David thought to himself, 'Saul will catch me someday. The best thing I can do is to escape to the land of the Philistines. Then Saul will give up looking for me in Israel. That way I will escape from Saul'" (1 Sam. 27:1 ERV).

Trusting God in his true identity of shepherd-poet-warrior-king, David is invincible. When he switches to asking himself for advice, he becomes fearful and decides to run. Self-protection and self-preservation are always the strategy of a fearful person and an indicator of the false self taking charge.

David decides to take his elite fighting force over to the Philistines and commence a life as a murderer, caravan robber, and liar. That's what he becomes in order to protect his life, even though Saul had pledged to stop pursuing David.

While he's doing that, what might his men be thinking and feeling? They know of David's reverence and trust in the Lord his God. Do they wonder about David's dramatic shift in strategy? "Wow, what happened to our fearless leader? Suddenly he's afraid, and we're running away from danger. One of us can kill eight hundred men. One of us can defeat an entire army, and we're robbing caravans? And we're lying and telling the Philistines that we're doing one thing when we're really over here doing something else, and we're murdering people and covering it up. This is what we've turned into? Is this what we do? What happened?"

David gave up his true identity and stepped into a false identity. Our shepherd-poet-warrior-king is now our liar-murderer-bandit-king.

Once while speaking with inmates in a correctional facility, I met a man who was a former soldier, decorated for his acts of heroism and bravery on the field of battle. "I prepared my whole life to be a soldier," he told me, his hands and feet manacled. "I went to military school as a kid and then straight into the service when I was old enough to apply. I was on my final tour of duty when something inside of me snapped. I don't know what it was, but I became consumed with the thought of death. In the location where I was deployed, there was easy access to opium, and this gave relief to my states of hypertension. Unfortunately, instead of seeking professional help, I relied on drugs and alcohol, and I was eventually discharged from the military. I later committed armed robbery to support my habit. If it wasn't for God, I'd probably be dead. It's crazy how fast it happened," he said, shaking his head. "It's like one moment you're a hero and the next minute a criminal."

When we take our eyes off Jesus, the author and perfecter of our faith,[6] we stop abiding and we become separate from truth. This separation results in a descent into falsehood. This descent, unchecked, whether gradual or rapid, is inevitable and often destructive.

David discovers the calamitous effect of his self-referential leadership when, on returning to their home camp in Ziklag, he and his men discover that an Amalekite raiding party has burned their camp and taken their wives and sons and daughters captive. David and his men are so overcome that they weep aloud until they have no strength left to weep. Then, bitter in spirit at the loss of their sons and daughters, David's men talk of stoning their once beloved leader.[7]

Suddenly, David's not so invincible anymore. Why? Because he stepped out of the identity that God gave him into a false identity of self-protection and self-promotion.

What is our safeguard against this kind of deadly thinking? We engage in this type of thinking every day. It's called walking side by side with ourself as our own counselor. It's a one-sided conversation that sounds something like this.

Jamie: What do you think about the situation you find yourself in?

Jamie: I'm afraid.

Jamie: I knew it. I'm afraid too.

Jamie: What are you going to do to protect yourself?

Jamie: I was planning on abandoning all hope and running away.

Jamie: Good plan. I'm all in because I think I'm a failure.

Jamie: I agree.

Of course, the enemy is willing to chime in.

Enemy: You are right. You are so wise. People aren't paying attention to the facts. They're stupid. You know you're going to lose this thing. When your mother said you were a loser, you knew she was right. Wasn't she right?

Jamie: Yeah, she was right.

This lie-based conversation is easy to believe because it never takes faith to believe what's false. Never. But it does take faith to believe what's true.

God wants to enter the conversation.

God: You're not in any danger. You never are.

That takes faith to believe.

God: "I am the Resurrection, and I am Life Eternal.
Anyone who clings to me in faith, even though
he dies, will live forever. And the one who lives
by believing in me will never die" (John 11:25–26
TPT).

Now that statement is hard to believe. In fact, we don't believe it at all. If we tell the truth, we believe this life is actually
better than the life to come. That's why we're always praying,
"God, don't let this person die. Please don't let them die." Why
are we saying that? Why are we praying that way?

My wife and I have two friends who are very close to physical death. They are great men, powerful men who have loved
God their entire lives.

One of them is now paralyzed from the neck down because
of a disease that's eaten through his spine. Physically, he cannot
move, and yet he is vibrant and powerful.

His wife called my wife, and Donna asked, "How's your
husband doing?"

She said, "Oh, he's driving me crazy. He keeps saying he can
see the river into the city, and he wants to put his foot in the
river, but he can't quite reach it. And he can see the trees on the
other side of the river in the city filled with fruit, and he's trying to reach out and take the fruit, but he can't quite reach it."

And you know what his wife said to her husband? She said,
"I'll help you put your foot in the river. Go, go, go, go."

Do you think of death like that? "Go. Run again. Be alive,
be free."

The other man is eighty-nine years old and deathly ill, but
he was able to get up and come into a meeting we were having.
He said, "I'm living . . . I'm in two worlds. I have a foot in both
worlds, and I don't want to waste any time over in this world. I
want to use it for all the value it has. There's beauty here, and
I want to pay attention to it. And yet, over there is my son."

His son had died when this man was twenty-seven years old.

"My son is over there, and I want to go see him," he said as he started crying.

He was not crying about dying. He wanted to get to the other side. "I want to see my son again. I want to go."

This is the way they view death. Scripture asks, "O death, where is your victory? O death, where is your sting?" (1 Cor. 15:55 ESV). Do we not believe this? If we're afraid to die, we will do anything to protect our lives.

Jesus makes us this cautionary promise: "All who are obsessed with being secure in life will lose it all—including their lives. But those who let go of their lives and surrender them to me will discover true life" (Luke 17:33 TPT).

Do you hear that promise? I've never seen it on a bookmark or poster displaying the promises of God. We should have this promise hanging on the refrigerator or on the bathroom mirror.

David stepped into false thinking and identity. He thought, *How does my world look?* And the news said it's bad. It's terrible. It's disastrous.

What can we do in a similar situation? We have withdrawn and shut down. We've lost our identity, and the people around us have begun to dislike us. We've become isolated even when in groups, and our communities won't help us. We've become a reproach because we're living in such fear and false identity.

We have got to come out of this deadly thinking and deal with the question of identity.

In "Attention," the first section of this book, we learned to tell our truth to God and then listen to God speak his truth back to us. This brings transformation.

By way of illustration, remember the trash pile metaphor? There are rats foraging around a trash pile, and you are tasked with getting rid of the rats. You can spend many futile hours trying to kill individual rats, but the rats will continue to come.

It's wiser and easier to simply get rid of the trash pile. No trash pile, no rats.

Our false identity is a trash pile that invites wrong belief in a myriad of lies. Trying to eliminate every lie we believe is time consuming and difficult. What is more effective is eliminating the false identity that attracts the lies and allows Satan a foothold into our spiritual life.

By thinking for himself rather than trusting God, David moved into a false self. He believed himself to be unloved and unprotected by God. Once he accepted this false view of himself, the lies came like rats to the trash pile to the point where David began living out the lies as truth. Even his own men considered killing him.

We're going to find our own trash pile, and that trash pile is a false identity. The process is very simple. The way to discover the false identity is to ask God to tell you what that false identity is.

This is what prayer is all about. Seeking and listening to God. This is why prayer is so effective and powerful.

As I pray, I'm going to ask God to search you and know you as in Psalm 139:23–24 and reveal to you the false names or false identities you believe to be true about yourself. These will be negative things people have called you or negative things you've called yourself throughout your life. You might know them already. Many of us do because we live in them all the time—we feel accused and condemned. It could be a long or a short list. The length doesn't matter.

When you hear or sense these false names or identities, I want you to write them down on something you can burn or tear up because we're not going to hold on to them. We're going to get rid of them.

Confession is telling the truth to God about what you believe about yourself that feels true. The only way that David could come out of the situation he was in with his men, who wanted to kill him, was to go back to his true identity. He could return to his true identity as quickly as he left it. You can do the same.

Let's listen and write.

Father, thank you for this reader. I bless them in the name of the Father, Son, and Holy Spirit.

Father, thank you for your Word. Thank you, Lord, for these men and women in history we can read about. They lived their lives on these pages so that we can see their mistakes, their fear, their guilt, their shame, and then, Lord, see how you reached in and redeemed and rescued them every time they called out to you. You were right there with them—as you are with us—because you love us, because you long for us to be with you as you are with us. This is your desire. We love you because you first loved us. We know that you love us because while we were sinners you died for us. This is how much you love us.

Lord, help us to know the truth of what we believe about ourselves. Lord, in the name of Jesus, I ask you again to clear our minds of other voices. We want to hear only you, Lord, just the voice of the true Lord Jesus, a voice that doesn't condemn and accuse but speaks only truth in love.

Lord, would you search us now with your Spirit? Would you search us and know us? Lord, would you tell us the false names and the false identities we believe to be true about ourselves? Bring them to our mind, Lord.

As the Lord brings these false names and identities to mind, write them down. Go ahead; don't be afraid. Let the Lord search you. We want this stuff cleared out. We want to be free.

Lord, search us all the way. Every secret room, every closed place in our heart. Lord, shine your light in there and show

*us any false thing, any false identity about ourselves that we
believe to be true.*

The reason you're writing it down is a tactical matter. These
false identities give the enemy a place to work in your life. Believing them gives authority to the enemy that he doesn't actually
have. We hand him the authority when we believe his accusations
and live from false identities. So write these out in front of the
spiritual world. We're putting the enemy on notice right now that
we're going to speak out the false identities. And we're doing it in
the presence of our King, our God, in his protection and safety.

Once you have written them down, I want you to use your
imagination, which is the place where you have dreams and visions. Your imagination is from God. Isaiah promises that the
one whose mind and imagination are committed to and focused
on God will be kept in perfect and constant peace by God.[8]

Instead of using our imagination to ruin ourselves, we're
going to use it the way God intended—to see thoughts and
ideas the way God sees them, to see the unseen reality.

*Father, would you sanctify our imagination right now, this
great gift you've given us, in order to picture all of the things
our imagination is for—things in the future, new ideas, new
inventions, a happy future? Lord, would you guide our imagination right now in your presence, in your holiness?*

Next, picture giving your list of false identities to Jesus.
Imagine this in your mind. The reason we're picturing Jesus
is because he is the exact representation of the invisible God.
When we see Jesus, we see the Father.

*Lord, guide us in this. Show us what it looks like when we
hand these false identities to you. Lord, show us what Jesus
does with these false identities when we hand them to him.*

87

Whatever you imagine or picture Jesus doing, I want you to remember it because I want you to describe it out loud. If you didn't see anything, it's okay. Just say, "I didn't see anything." Always tell the truth.

After a few seconds, I want you to share what you pictured. Confession time with Jesus and one another is freeing. This is what God intended.

When Jesus went to Zacchaeus's house, Zacchaeus was filled with joy that Jesus came to be with him. Zacchaeus is the one who came up with the idea of returning four times the amount of money he had taken illegally.[9] Jesus didn't tell him to do it. Being with Jesus, transformed into his true identity, Zacchaeus did what his true identity knew to do. He returned what he had stolen and began to live generously.

Zacchaeus had been hoarding money, living 180 degrees opposite of his true identity. When he met Jesus, he moved into his true identity and gave money away.

When Jesus interacted with people, he didn't ask them to apologize. He did something more powerful and liberating to the human spirit. Jesus demanded truth telling. Consider 1 John 1:9: "If we [freely] admit that we have sinned and confess our sins, He is faithful and just [true to His own nature and promises], and will forgive our sins and cleanse us continually from all unrighteousness [our wrongdoing, everything not in conformity with His will and purpose]" (AMP).

Confession (Greek, *homologeō*—"to agree with, assent, not to deny") results in God's forgiveness (Greek, *aphiēmi*—"to send away") of our sins (Greek, *hamartia*—"missing the mark, wandering from the path of uprightness").

Jesus did not create an embezzling tax collector. He created a man who knew how to make money and give it away, more even than what the law required. Zacchaeus does this and he's filled with joy—and so is everyone around him.

When we come to the Lord with a false identity, it should be the happiest moment of our life. "Jesus, I admit and agree that I am living a lie. Here, Jesus, take these false things and do with them whatever you want. I don't want them any longer."

Once that house has been swept clean, we don't want to leave it empty. Otherwise, the lies will come back and we don't want that.[10]

If you saw Jesus do something with the false names and identities you wrote down, do what you saw. Or throw them in a trash can, rip them up, spit on them, burn them, whatever feels right to you. But get rid of them. We're done with those things. We don't want them anymore. We're going to move into our new identity. We're going to start making plans out of the new, true, unique-to-you identity.

Father, thank you for this reader. I bless them in the name of the Father, Son, and Holy Spirit.

Lord, thank you for their truthfulness. God, thank you for being a God who pursues us with truth and true identity. You made us to be something. We want to be real with you, tell you the truth, and move into our true identity with you. Thank you for your forgiveness. Thank you for your kindness that leads us to repentance. It's never condemnation; it's never guilt. It's kindness that leads to freedom! We're going to be done with these names and stop acting in these false identities. So, Lord, we give them to you, and we ask that you close the door on them. Lord, teach us to live in our true identity. In Jesus's name, amen.

PART 3

ANNUNCIATION

Listen and hear my voice; pay attention and hear what I say.

ISAIAH 28:23 NIV

For the Word that God speaks is alive and full of
power . . . ; it is sharper than any two-edged sword.

HEBREWS 4:12

Once, after a particularly devastating setback in a Middle Eastern country that resulted in our arrest and expulsion from that
country, a friend called to check on our well-being and offer
encouragement. After listening to me recount the circumstances
surrounding the event—the betrayal, the failure, and the resulting sense of fear, guilt, and shame—his advice was simple:
"Well, God still speaks and his word still cuts, so let's ask God
what he wants you to know and what he wants you to do."

God still speaks and his word still cuts—two often-neglected
facts that help protect us from bad decisions, wrong conclusions,

and just overall faulty thinking. Let's consider each truth in turn.

If Only You'd Asked

How often do we forget the astounding truth that we worship the God who speaks?

At that seemingly inescapable low point in my walk with the Lord, being arrested and expelled from a country, I remembered the words of James, the brother of Jesus, in his letter to the Jews who were *dispersed* throughout the non-Jewish world: "If any of you is deficient in wisdom, let him ask of the giving God [Who gives] to everyone liberally and ungrudgingly, without reproaching or faultfinding, and it will be given him" (James 1:5).

Deficient in wisdom? I feel as if I'm regularly lacking in wisdom. What's the solution? Ask. And please note that the one you are asking is no distant, petulant, capricious god of our own invention that cannot help and leads us astray.[1] Instead, we are calling on the One who spoke creation—that includes us—into existence and calls us by name. This is the God of Abraham, Isaac, and Jacob, the God and Father of our Lord Jesus Christ, who gives wisdom (Greek, *sophia*—"broad and full of intelligence; used of the knowledge of very diverse matters") liberally without reproach or faultfinding.

God is ready and willing to lavish his wisdom all over us if we will only ask. In addition to his willingness to pour out this wisdom, God's wisdom covers every discipline of human endeavor. We need only inquire of him.

In 1961, Indiana University Press published the now classic work *Ecstasy: A Study of Some Secular and Religious Experiences*, wherein author Marghanita Laski outlines a six-step process underlying "eureka" breakthroughs—creative insights, revelations, and transformations of mind that change the course of science, philosophy, art, or religion.[2] From Aristotle to Einstein, Beethoven to the Beatles, cave etchings to Cézanne, all human creativity and innovation begins with a simple action: ask a question.

What about Jesus in his humanity? How did Jesus know things?

The Gospel writer Luke relates a fascinating incident wherein the young Jesus, who has grown and become strong and is filled with wisdom and the grace of God (Luke 2:40), has now reached the important age of twelve. At this point, a boy is supposed to enter that period of life when having learned the requirements of the law through his parents' instruction he now takes on the responsibility himself. This rite, which is still in existence, consists in the preparation by the candidate of certain passages of the law, which are to be recited and presented to rulers and doctors. At that time, they may ask him questions, testing his knowledge, and he may submit to them questions arising out of his training.

As dutiful Jews, Mary and Joseph would have prepared the boy for this significant event and celebrated the monumental occasion in Jerusalem. However, upon their travels back home within the caravan, Mary and Joseph discover the young lad to be missing. After three days of frantic searching, the understandably upset parents locate their son, who had remained in the courts of the temple, sitting among the teachers, listening and asking them questions (v. 46).

This prompts Mary to ask her son a question: "Child, why have You treated us like this?" (v. 48). Mary's request for an explanation seems self-focused and accusatory and not a request for any real wisdom or insight. She is faultfinding.

The boy Jesus, however, asks a tender and respectful question in return that offers wisdom and understanding to his mother. "How is it that you had to look for Me? Did you not see and know that it is necessary [as a duty] for Me to be in My Father's house and [occupied] about My Father's business?" (v. 49). At a culturally and religiously appropriate age, Jesus is listening and asking questions to both discover and impart the wisdom of his Father. Mary needs to be reminded of the plan of God in the birth of Jesus. She needs wisdom and understanding about her divine child. Jesus will never disobey or mistreat his parents; however, he will be obedient to his heavenly Father above all else. Mary receives this reminder and "persistently guarded all these things in her heart" (v. 51). As for Jesus, he "increased in wisdom (in broad and full understanding) and in stature and years, and in favor with God and man" (v. 52).

Jesus, being a fully human youth, grew in wisdom, which included asking questions and seeking the guidance of human parents and teachers, but then he grew into the fullness of his identity by seeking wisdom and guidance directly from the Father himself. Certainly, after his baptism in the Jordan River when God publicly identified him as the beloved Son in whom he is well pleased,[3] Jesus, filled with the Holy Spirit,[4] moved at a level of wisdom.

Is this not a process for us to understand and engage? Consider Jesus's words:

> I am able to do nothing from Myself [independently, of My own accord—but only as I am taught by God and as I get His orders]. Even as I hear, I judge [I decide as I am bidden to decide. As the voice comes to Me, so I give a decision], and My judgment is right (just, righteous), because I do not seek or consult My own will . . . but only the will and pleasure of the Father Who sent Me. (John 5:30)

Jesus is modeling for humanity the highest level of knowing— asking wisdom from the God who speaks!

Think of it from this perspective: Jesus isn't so much teaching people what to do in a given situation as he is teaching them *how to know what to do in every situation*—ask and keep on asking, seek and keep on seeking, knock and keep on knocking.[5]

Surely the disciples of Jesus had begun to realize that Jesus's way of knowing was beyond anything they'd ever experienced. How did Jesus always seem to know where to go, who to meet, when to start talking, what to say, when to stop talking, when to leave, who to take with him, who to leave behind, who to raise from the dead, who not to raise from the dead, when to break with Jewish laws, when not to break with Jewish laws, and so on? Perhaps this is the motivation in Luke 11:1 when, after seeing Jesus pray (again!) in a certain place, one of the disciples said, "Lord, teach us to pray, just as John taught his disciples" (NIV). Scripture doesn't tell us how or what John taught his disciples, but Luke associates prayer with the most important moments of Jesus's life: Jesus prays at his baptism and after a day of working miracles; Jesus spends the night in prayer before choosing the Twelve; Jesus prays alone before Peter's confession of faith and Jesus's first reference to the cross; Jesus prays on the mountain where he is transfigured; and Jesus rejoices in prayer after the mission of the seventy-two because of the Father's revelation to his children.[6] After witnessing Jesus's constant communication with the Father and the ensuing results, a normal person has got to ask, "Can you teach me to do that?"

I suspect that Jesus, being a teacher par excellence, is waiting for this question. It doesn't matter that it took the disciples eleven chapters to ask, Jesus is ready to dispense his prayer wisdom liberally and without reproach. Of course, his teaching is not what they expect. He says in so many words, "When you pray, you need to do so in a different way from what you might have observed in others or been taught as observant Jews. Don't be like the hypocrites who make a big show of prayer for all to see, and don't be like the pagans who think more words equal more results.[7] Rather, when you pray, think about it like this: God is actually Father to you. He's in heaven, and he is above all. You must come to him as Father."

That's how Jesus taught. Here's how we process it today: "Our Father, who art in heaven." We made it a memorized prayer. It takes the least amount of thought. Rote memory doesn't require us to think deeply, and more importantly, it doesn't require relationship. We simply repeat it over and over again.

Jesus knew our tendency to turn things into a formula and make them a ritual. That's what we do to avoid relationship.

Speaking again on the topic of prayer, Jesus said that the Father knows what we need before we ask him.[8] What does that tell us about how we should pray? How does it inform our prayer life? What should we be asking God? Perhaps when we pray, we should ask, "Lord, what do I need?"

There's your prayer life. If the Father knows what you need before you ask him, why don't you ask him what you need? If you ask him what you need and he tells you what you need, then pray for that. Your prayer will always be answered—without fail.

When each of our three sons were born, we dedicated them to the Lord. We asked God daily to make clear to us throughout their lives what they needed to become who he intended them to be: "Lord, give us wisdom today, as parents entrusted with the stewardship of this God-formed, unique identity, show us what this child needs this day to grow in wisdom and stature and favor with both you and others."

The answer to that request for parenting wisdom from God was not to "hide them away in the safest place you can and teach them to self-promote and self-protect and avoid strangers and dangers at any cost." It was quite the opposite. As C. S. Lewis writes of the Christ-character, Aslan, in The Chronicles of Narnia: "Safe? Who said anything about safe? 'Course he isn't safe. But he's good. He's the King, I tell you."[9]

What God had in mind for our sons was that they grow up in the Muslim world, learning to love and share their faith with the sons and daughters of Ishmael. Believe me, that is not what my wife and I had in mind, but we are so grateful for the fine global friends, husbands, and fathers they have become.

Ask the Father, "God, what do I need today? What do you say I need?" What you need is probably not what you think. In his humanity, Jesus modeled praying in this way. He constantly sought the wisdom and guidance of his heavenly Father. Scripture records Jesus praying twenty-five different times during his earthly ministry.

Jesus knows how to know what to do, and his way of knowing is by being in a dialogical, love relationship with his Father, the God who speaks.

In a Muslim country where we once lived, I had a student named Salim[10] who needed a driver's license to secure a profitable job to help provide for his ailing parents. The challenge for Salim was that because he was a member of a discriminated ethnic minority, obtaining a government-issued driver's license was nearly impossible.

"I've tried three times," he told me, exasperated with the process. "I go to the government office, wait in line for hours, and if they call my name, which they've only done once, as soon as they see my ethnicity, they reject my application."

Salim and I had only been meeting together for a few months, but we were quite deep in studying the people of the Scriptures. "What did Moses and Gideon do when they faced situations that seemed impossible?" I asked Salim. "How about the Samaritan woman alone at the well? Who helped her?"

"They asked God for wisdom," he replied. "But does God know how to get a driver's license from a corrupt government? Plus, even if I get to take the test, I don't have much experience driving. Can God give me real-time driving instructions, or does God do just religious stuff?"

How many of us think God does only *religious stuff*? Sure, God can help us with religious issues, but what does he know about real life—you know, the Monday-through-Friday grind in a hostile, broken world? As a result of this type of thinking, we simply do not ask God for wisdom in significant areas of our lives. I would never have understood the depths of God's wisdom regarding police work if I had not asked him what he knew about working homicides, domestic disputes, and armed robberies and loving defense attorneys. Turned out, the Lord knows quite a bit about literally everything. James, the brother of Jesus, says plainly, "You do not have because you do not ask" (James 4:2 NIV).

Is That a Fake ID?

Not asking is one hindrance to our journey of hearing the voice of God in our lives. But there is another, I think more insidious, impediment to receiving God's guidance: trying to listen from within a false sense of self—a false identity.

Therefore, it is important to understand that the word (Greek, *logos*—"word uttered by a living voice") God speaks is able to penetrate "as far as the division of the soul and spirit [the completeness of a person], and of both joints and marrow [the deepest parts of our nature], exposing and judging the very thoughts and intentions of the heart. And not a creature exists that is concealed from His sight, but all things are open and exposed, and revealed to the eyes of Him with whom we have to give account" (Heb. 4:12–13 AMP).

God's Word cuts through all the lies we believe about God, ourselves, others, and the world and moves us toward truth. Without this revelation, either we don't ask at all, or we ask with "wrong motives [out of selfishness or with an unrighteous agenda]" (James 4:3 AMP), or we ask in doubt, wavering "like a billowing surge of the sea that is blown about and tossed by the wind. For such a person ought not to think or expect that he will receive anything [at all] from the Lord, being a double-minded man, unstable and restless in all his ways [in everything he thinks, feels, or decides]" (James 1:6–8 AMP).

I challenged Salim: "Let's pray and ask God what he wants you to know about getting a driver's license. Then just listen and write down what you sense from the Lord."

At this point in his life, Salim was not a follower of Jesus, but he had a deep reverence for God and prayer. Like Cornelius, the Roman centurion in Acts 10, Salim, a Muslim, longed to know the truth of Jesus and the kingdom of God.

After several minutes but what seemed like hours, Salim wrote down in his journal: "I am afraid. I am a failure. I am a disappointment."

Isn't it interesting that the first words God communicated to Salim when he asked what God wanted him to know about obtaining a driver's license were very deep and cutting words about what Salim believed about himself?

You cannot know God in any deep way from a false identity. You just can't. Satan's desire, whether you believe in Satan or not, is that you live your life making guesses, mostly wrong, about who you are, who God is, and who your neighbor is. You end up guessing your way through life and doing the best you can. That's one way to live—most people do it that way—but it's not a great way to live. You might survive with this strategy, but you will not thrive.

There is, however, an alternative way of knowing, in which you can know at a much higher level the things about this world and beyond. You can make decisions in the present, knowing more than you can see right at this moment. That's what Jesus teaches.

God begins with identity: "They will call him Immanuel, which means 'God is with us'" (Matt. 1:23 NLT).

In his humanness, Jesus received his identity from the Father and only moved according to the will of God: "Father, if you are willing, take this cup of agony away from me. But no matter what, your will must be mine" (Luke 22:42 TPT). Simultaneously, in the mystery of Jesus's divinity, he is "the dazzling radiance of God's splendor, the exact expression of God's true nature—his mirror image! He holds the universe together and expands it by the mighty power of his spoken word. He accomplished for us the complete cleansing of sins, and then took his seat on the highest throne at the right hand of the majestic One" (Heb. 1:3 TPT).

In Paul's letter to the Colossians, he speaks of Jesus in this way: "He is the divine portrait, the true likeness of the invisible God, and the firstborn heir of all creation" (Col. 1:15 TPT).

In Jesus, the human and divine natures, though ever distinct, are united in one person by the hypostatic union.[11] What this means for us as ones created in the image of God is astounding and breathtaking.

On the one hand, as discussed earlier, we see Jesus in his humanity gaining wisdom and direction from the Father through dialogical relationship. We, as humans, can also engage in this same dialogical relationship, resulting in our transformation.

On the other hand, and this is a staggering truth, Jesus in his divinity is God incarnate interacting with humanity. Jesus says this simply and directly when Philip asks him to show them the Father: "Philip, I've been with you all this time and you still don't know who I am? How could you ask me to show you the Father, for anyone who has looked at me has seen the Father" (John 14:9 TPT).

Did you get that? Through Jesus's life, we are in essence seeing how God walks and talks with humans in all kinds of situations. In fact, Jesus is the lens through which to view *all* of

Scripture. According to the great reformer Martin Luther, "The Scriptures must be understood in favor of Christ, not against him. For that reason, they must either refer to him or must not be held to be true Scriptures."[12] With this understanding from the New Testament, Luther, like many other interpreters in the early church, understood appearances of the God of Israel in the Old Testament as appearances of the Son.[13]

> It follows cogently and incontrovertibly that the God who led the children of Israel from Egypt and through the Red Sea, who guided them in the wilderness by means of the pillar of cloud and pillar of fire, who nourished them with bread from heaven, who performed all the miracles recorded by Moses in his books, again, who brought them into the land of Canaan and there gave them kings and priest and everything, is the very same God, and none other than Jesus of Nazareth, the Son of the Virgin Mary, whom we Christians call our Lord and God.

> Likewise, it is He who gave Moses the Ten Commandments on Mount Sinai, saying (Exod. 20:2, 3), "I am the Lord your God who led you out of Egypt . . . you shall have no other gods before Me." Yes, Jesus of Nazareth, who died for us on the cross, is the God who says in the first commandment, "I, the Lord, am your God."[14]

Do What? Are You Talking to Me?

From beginning to end, Scripture is brimming with conversations between the Creator and his creation. From Adam in Genesis to the apostle John in Revelation, God is speaking to humanity. Let's look at three examples and then see how God might interact with Salim in his quest for a driver's license.

Most Christians are familiar with the story of Moses and his encounter with the Word incarnate in the form of a burning bush described in Exodus 3. In this dialogical interchange, which is initiated by God, between the human and the divine, God speaks the truth of God's identity—I AM WHO I AM[15]—to Moses and calls Moses into the truth of who Moses is—the one sent to bring Israel out of Egypt. Scripture tells us that God spoke to Moses face-to-face as we would speak to a friend.[16]

If we had encountered Moses one day (or even one hour) prior to his dialogue with the divine and had asked him about his identity, he might have responded that he was a shepherd. If he really trusted us, he might have confessed that he was an exiled criminal, wanted in Egypt for murder. Notice though that when God speaks to Moses, he does not call Moses the names the accuser(s) calls him. When Moses asks, "Who am I that I should go?" (v. 11 NIV), God's response is one of promise and blessing: "I will be with you" (v. 12 NIV). Even when Moses gets down to his deeper confession of how he views his *real self*, that he is not very good with words and has a tendency to get tongue-tied, which may lead to the people not believing or listening to him, God gives him wisdom on how to proceed. But please notice that the words God is speaking to Moses cut deep into the very depths of what Moses believes about God, himself, his own people, the world of the Egyptians, and beyond. Finally, fears fully exposed by the initiating, incarnate, wisdom-giving God who speaks, Moses is left with a choice: obey or disobey, say yes or no.

It's important to understand the meaning of the Hebrew word *sh'ma* (שָׁמַע), which is the title of one of Judaism's most sacred prayers found in Deuteronomy 6:4–9. Pious Jews hope to die with the words of the Shema on their lips. The word *sh'ma* in Deuteronomy 6:4 is translated "hear," and this is correct. However, the word *sh'ma* can also be translated into the English word *obey*, which can cause the Hebraic idea of listening to God to be reduced to the idea of following a list of codified rules and regulations apart from a living, dialogical relationship with the God who speaks.

There is no Hebrew word meaning "obey"; neither is there an English word for שמע. While this Hebrew verb is often translated as "hear," it means much more than just hearing or listening but rather to "hear and respond appropriately." When the Bible says that Moses "heard" YHWH, it means that he heard him and then he acted on what he heard. When the Bible says that YHWH "heard" the people, it means that he heard them and then acted on what he heard.[17]

So when we talk about obeying God, let's think beyond rule following to hearing God and responding appropriately. Of course, it stands to reason that if we're not listening to God, it's difficult to respond appropriately.

Moses is listening to God and asking questions, but ultimately he responds with, "Please my Lord, send the message [of rescue to Israel] by [someone else]" (Exod. 4:13 AMP).

Get this, reader! The God of Abraham, Isaac, and Jacob, the great I AM, announces to his friend Moses that his identity is the one sent to draw Israel out of bondage, and Moses responds, "Send somebody else."

If we could pull Moses aside for a moment and ask, "What emotion is driving your decision-making process right now?" I'm guessing he would answer like most of us and say fear grounded in shame. Moses might remind us of his last failed attempt at rescuing just one of his own Hebrew countrymen from an oppressive Egyptian[18] and of his forty years in exile as a murderer. He went from a position of power and authority in the greatest kingdom of the day to being a sheep watcher at "the backside [lit. the part *after the following part*[19]] of the desert" (Exod. 3:1 KJV). Now he's supposed to go deliver the entire nation? Get real!

But God is not offering this annunciation of invitation to Moses so he'll get real but so he'll get true! Jesus says, "If you

. . . [live] out what I tell you . . . you will experience for yourselves the truth, and the truth will free you" (John 8:32 MSG).

Moses really did make a mistake by moving to help his people without first asking God for wisdom. This real mistake had real consequences that cannot be denied or ignored. But this mistake did not steal Moses's God-given identity and replace it with an identity of failure and shame. God's appearance and words to Moses are restoring Moses to who he has always been—a friend and a deliverer of a nation.

Scripture tells us that when Moses heard and responded inappropriately to God's invitation, God's anger flared.[20] God, in his great love for us, will never tolerate our believing the lies constantly being offered up to us by our own flesh, the world, and the Liar. These lies prevent us from understanding the truth about ourselves, and as we see with Moses, his false view of himself prevents him from hearing and responding appropriately to the One who created him.

In what ways is your false view of yourself, however real the mistakes you've made in the past, diminishing your capacity to hear and respond appropriately to the God who calls you by name and whose Word is ready to slice through all the lies you've come to believe about yourself?

In spite of Moses's inappropriate response, God in his kindness suggests Moses's elder brother, Aaron, as a person to walk alongside him in his challenging task. Moses hears the words of God and responds appropriately.

In his work *The Sickness Unto Death*, Danish philosopher Søren Kierkegaard explains that the most common form of human despair is not being who you are.[21] Consider the tragic self-identification of a generation of Israelites, who had witnessed God's miraculous presence and provision under the leadership of Moses, when they looked with fear on the inhabitants of the land promised to them by God: "We were *in our own sight* as grasshoppers, and so we were in their sight" (Num. 13:33 KJV, emphasis added).

In Judges 6, we see a conversation comparable to that of Moses and God in the encounter between the angel of the Lord and a very cautious young man named Gideon. Like the Mosaic scenario, Gideon finds himself and his people on the bottom rung of a world committed to climbing the ladder of power and acquisition at the cost of everyone less fortunate. As a result of seven years of pillaging by the Midianites, the impoverished (brought low) Israelites call out to the Lord for help. Interestingly, as a result of their cry, God first sends a prophet to the people. Then the angel of the Lord appears to a fainthearted farmer thrashing wheat in a cave for fear of marauding Midianites.

As in the conversation with Moses, the angel of the Lord initiates the encounter with Gideon and announces two truths Gideon is quite ready to dispute. The spoken words cut to the core of Gideon's wrong beliefs about God, himself, and the world around him.

First, Gideon is informed that Jehovah, meaning "the existing One," is with him (v. 12). Gideon's response is, in effect, "God might have been with us in olden days, but he has abandoned us in the present day."

Second, Gideon is informed that his identity with God is "mighty man of [fearless] courage" (v. 12) and that he already possesses the great strength necessary to deliver Israel from her enemies. Gideon's response to this information is "my clan is the poorest in Manasseh, and I am the least in my father's house" (v. 15).

As with Moses, the loving God who speaks is willing to walk Gideon from the false to the true, from the lie of abandonment to the truth of I AM is with you and I AM is sending you in your true identity as the mighty man of courage destined to set his people free. As David Benner writes, "We do not find our true self by seeking it. Rather, we find it by seeking God."[22]

Gideon, for his part, listens to the words of God and responds appropriately. He does so with fear and trepidation, but that's okay; it's a journey.

The writer of Hebrews tells us that "in these last days" God has "spoken to us by his Son, whom he appointed the heir of all things, through whom also he created the world" (1:2 ESV). With this in mind, let's consider a conversation with the Creator Son from the Gospel of John.

Come See the One!

In John 4, there is a remarkable account of Jesus's encounter with a Samaritan woman in a town called Sychar in Samaria. She has come alone at midday to draw water from a famous well located on a plot of ground that, according to tradition, the patriarch Jacob gave to his son Joseph. The ensuing conversation, initiated by the wearied Word incarnate himself with the imperative "Give Me a drink" (v. 7 AMP), is described by St. Augustine as one "full of mysteries and pregnant with sacraments."[23]

For our purposes, however, let's focus on the words of Jesus as they relate to sharing wisdom with this unique woman and the effect these words have in cutting away the false beliefs she has regarding God, herself, and the world around her.

The Jews and Samaritans had a long and contentious history.[24] We learn something about this woman's worldview when she responds to Jesus's request for water: "How is it that You, being a Jew, ask me, a Samaritan woman, for a drink? (For Jews have nothing to do with Samaritans)" (v. 9 AMP).

Whatever emotion this woman is feeling at this moment, and I'm guessing it's a mixed bag from insult to interest, she makes it clear that she knows the cultural categories and that the categories don't mix. For whatever reason, this woman doesn't even mix with other women when drawing water from a community well. She, like many of us today, exists within a separation worldview, sourced in scarcity, and thereby committed to a life of self-protection.

Do we separate people into categories? The word *category* is from the Greek word *kategoros* that means "to accuse." Revelation 12:10 names Satan as "the accuser of our brethren." Do we categorize people rather than affirm the beauty and uniqueness of God's creation?

As with Moses and Gideon, the Lord's desire here is to lead this "image of God" woman into the truth of who she is by revealing the truth of who he is in order that she might deliver her people from a life of bondage. He accomplishes this by cutting to the very core of her fear, guilt, and shame: "If you had only known and had recognized God's gift and Who this is that is saying to you, Give Me a drink, you would have asked Him [instead] and He would have given you living water" (John 4:10).

Although Jesus began the conversation by asking the woman to serve him (which she does not do), he breaks cultural convention by not responding to the separation categories named by the woman and instead offers to serve her. Why does Jesus do this? Because "the Son of Man came not to be served but to serve others and to give his life as a ransom for many" (Matt. 20:28 NLT).

How otherworldly is this idea? The king came to serve humanity. He came to serve you.

Take a moment and visualize Jesus standing before you, offering to serve you. Would you let him? Or would you be like Peter who, when Jesus offered to wash his feet, refused: "You shall never wash my feet" (John 13:8 NIV).

Jesus's response to Peter's refusal was strong: "Unless I wash you, you have no part with me" (v. 8 NIV).

In what ways are you refusing to let the Lord serve you? We must be willing recipients of all that God has for us. If we cannot or will not receive from the Lord, we cannot be partakers with him in all that he has for us. Furthermore, Jesus's service to us is in order that we will turn and serve others: "If I then, your Lord and Teacher (Master), have washed your feet, you ought [it is your duty, you are under obligation, you owe it] to wash one another's feet. For I have given you this as an example, so that you should do [in your turn] what I have done to you" (vv. 14–15).

Imagine our using this strategy! Instead of entering a religiously, culturally, ethnically, and politically tense situation and trying to overpower and subdue our enemies, we humble ourselves to the role of a servant and offer our very lives for their good. The apostle Paul says it this way: "For though I am free from all men, I have made myself a slave to everyone, so that I may win more [for Christ]" (1 Cor. 9:19 AMP).

The woman of Samaria is being guided into a level of wisdom and knowing she has never experienced, and she struggles to keep up. She wonders how Jesus can serve her without a bucket and further wonders if Jesus considers himself greater than their ancestor Jacob.[25]

But Jesus continues to move her to a higher level of understanding: "Everyone who drinks this water will be thirsty again. But whoever drinks the water that I give him will never be thirsty again. But the water that I give him will become in him a spring of water [satisfying his thirst for God] welling up [continually flowing, bubbling within him] to eternal life" (John 4:13–14 AMP).

I think it is fascinating to note here that the Samaritan people were hopeful for Messiah to come to them[26] and that Messiah was associated with "living water." Consider the following Samaritan texts known in the time of Jesus:

> *There is a Well of living water*
> *dug by a Prophet whose like has not arisen since Adam*

and the water which is in it is from the mouth of God.
Let us eat from the fruit that is in this garden
and let us drink from the waters that are in this well.[27]

In the depths of an abundant spring is the life of the
world.
Let us rise with understanding to drink from its waters!
We thirst for the waters of life.[28]

Whether these texts were known to the woman or not, she implores Jesus: "Sir, give me this water, so that I may never get thirsty" (v. 15), to which Jesus says to her to go get her husband.

Uh oh. What? Jesus is not going to just give her some magic words to say or zap her with some otherworldly water? No. He is leading her into *all* truth in order that she can be completely free. Jesus is the light that shines into those dark and hidden areas of our lives that prevent us from fully hearing, knowing, and receiving from him.

She makes an attempt at truth telling/confession with "I have no husband," which Jesus affirms, but then he cuts deeper into her darkness with the full light of truth: "You have spoken truly in saying, I have no husband. For you have had five husbands, and the man you are now living with is not your husband. In this you have spoken truly" (vv. 17–18).

I love how the truth telling speeds up once the woman has nothing else to conceal about herself. She now has the freedom to question a Jewish prophet, since the Jewish prophet is offering to serve her even knowing every diccy thing about her. She can now question the categories!

Here is my paraphrase of how the conversation proceeds: "Now that I get that you're a living-water-talking prophet, and a Jewish one at that, and you don't seem to have a problem venturing into Samaria to talk to a woman in my situation, let me ask you a question that has divided Jews and Samaritans for generations." She takes a deep breath while Jesus waits patiently. "Our theological experts teach us the only legit place to worship God is on Mount Gerizim, while your team says that Jerusalem is the only real-deal location for worship. Who is right?"

Jesus, the reconciler of humanity, smiles and explains, "The time is coming when the location of worship won't be so divisive because the location won't matter. Up until now, your people have not fully understood what you are worshiping, and that's why I'm excited to be talking to you. My people do have an understanding of what we are worshiping because the salvation of the world will come from among the Jewish people." Jesus pauses to let her consider his words. "However," he continues, "the time has come, when true worshipers, without categories, will worship the Father in spirit and in truth because God is Spirit and is therefore seeking those who will worship him in spirit and truth."

How beautiful are these words to a discouraged and disconnected person and world?

Perhaps Jesus's words and actions remind the woman of the Samaritan hope for *Taheb* (Messiah), "the Restorer who will return,"[29] spoken of in Samaritan literature and the Samaritan version of Torah.

She tells Jesus, "I know that Messiah is coming, He Who is called the Christ (the Anointed One); . . . He will tell us everything we need to know and make it clear to us" (v. 25).

Oh, she's ready now! Look how beautifully Jesus crossed all the boundaries to enter her lonely, isolated world to serve her. Look how he gently walked her into truth telling, which freed her to ask the questions that might have been troubling her mind for years. Look how Jesus's words of wisdom cut through the lies, allowing this woman to become who she truly is.

Imagine how surprised, overjoyed, shocked, and relieved this amazing woman is at the annunciation of Jesus: "I Who now speak with you am He" (v. 26).

The Messiah has come to reconcile Jews and Samaritans, men and women within the love of the Father, who seeks those who will worship him in spirit and truth.

Like the examples of Moses and Gideon, the woman hears the words of Messiah and responds appropriately. No longer willing to live in isolation and separateness, she hurries to the town and tells the people, "Come, see a Man Who has told me everything that I ever did! Can this be [is not this] the Christ? [Must not this be the Messiah, the Anointed One?]" (v. 29).

In the course of one afternoon with the Word incarnate, a woman trapped in a stultifying life of detachment and dejection becomes a person of influence, whose courageous witness leads a town of people—who might well have mistreated her—to faith in Christ.

Today, this woman's image is painted on the wall of the Samaritan Museum on Mount Gerizim. She is not only commemorated in Scripture but also honored and remembered to this day in her homeland.[30]

Why? Because she let the King serve her by walking with her from her false identity into her true identity in the kingdom of God.

How's your afternoon going?

The Cat in the Hat

My Muslim friend Salim looked at me with a furrowed brow. "What does God want me to know about thinking I'm a disappointment and a failure?"

"I think God wants you to know what the real hindrance is to you obtaining a driver's license," I said. "It's not the unfair policies of the government. God can overcome any obstacle. What God will not do is lead you with a false sense or belief of who you are and who he is. And he wants you to love the people who work in the government office, whether they give you a license or not."

111

Salim agreed to a spiritual exercise. He spent time each day confessing his wrong belief that he was a failure and disappointment in life, asking *Al-Masih* (Arabic, "Messiah") to lift the false identity from him and asking God to speak to him through *Ruh Al-Qudus* ("Holy Spirit") about his true identity.

After several weeks, Salim confessed to me that his identity as a failure and disappointment came from his poor performance in university. However, as he gave this false sense of himself to Messiah, he sensed the words *intellectual* and *scholar* from the Holy Spirit. We read Scripture to help confirm the process of listening to God and receiving our identity from God. The Bible became more alive to Salim as the words that God was speaking to him through the text and the Spirit brought light to the deep fears and insecurities of his heart.

One day, Salim said, "Let's ask God about getting a driver's license."

With his listening journal at the ready, Salim asked God for wisdom: "Whatever you say, Lord, I will listen and respond."

Very quickly Salim wrote down in his journal, "Don't be afraid. Go stand in line at the licensing office. I AM is with you."

"That sounds like God to me," I said encouragingly.

Early the next morning, Salim went to stand in line. After six hours, a police officer called his name. Salim asked God for strength, approached the police officer, and handed him his ID, fully expecting the officer—a member of the ruling ethnic majority and enemy of Salim's people—to reject his application outright. Astonishingly, the police officer ordered Salim to enter the vehicle for the driving test.

At this point, Salim was terrified because he was a very inexperienced driver, and he had never sat in such close proximity to a person whose people had done so much to destroy Salim's family and people. The police officer was his worst enemy.

"Drive," the officer instructed, and Salim was grateful to sense quite powerfully the presence of God with him in the vehicle. "Love your enemy," the words of Messiah soothed him. "Do good to those who hate you." Salim drove on, becoming more relaxed with every minute.

Then he saw the cat.

The cat, lying injured on the side of the road, looked as if it had been struck by a car. Salim felt very strongly that the Lord wanted him to stop and help the cat.

"I can't," he whispered to God. "The policeman will become angry and will fail me."

Salim stopped the car at a red traffic signal but could not stop the words that burst forth from his mouth. "Sir, I think we should go back and help the injured cat."

"What do you care about a stray cat?" the policeman snapped.

"I believe God wants us to help the injured animal." Salim winced at his own words. "God loves cats too."

"Well, if your God is telling you to turn around," the police-man huffed, "you'd better obey."

Salim whipped the car into a legal U-turn and returned to the injured but still living animal. Both Salim and the officer stood staring at the cat for a moment until the officer asked, "What should we do?"

"Do you have a box or something in the trunk of your car?" asked Salim.

"I have a blanket. We could lay the cat on a blanket and take it to a vet."

"That sounds like a good idea, sir," Salim agreed.

"But how do we pick the cat up? I don't want to touch it with my hands," said the officer.

Salim asked God for wisdom. "Can we use your hat?"

"What?" said the policeman, incredulous.

"Your hat. Can we scoop the cat up in your hat and lay it on the blanket in the trunk? I will clean your hat for you later. My cousin works in a laundromat. Many of my people work in laundromats because without licenses we cannot get good-paying jobs. I will get your hat cleaned for you."

"You will clean my police hat?"

"Cleaner than it has ever been before. Let's save the cat."

Salim and the officer knelt down and working together were able to scoop the skeletal-like cat into the policeman's hat. They worked together to lay the cat gently on a blanket in the car's trunk.

With the cat secure, the officer said with some haste to Salim, "You drive. I'll give directions to the vet. Drive as fast as you can and disregard traffic signals. This is an emergency."

As if in a dream, Salim drove quickly and safely through the city, urged onward by his onetime enemy turned feline-rescuing compatriot. Bound together in a quest to save the life of a stray cat, Salim and the officer paced the waiting room of the veterinary clinic together, hoping against hope that their efforts were not in vain. When the vet burst forth and announced that the cat would live another day, Salim and the officer hugged and complimented one another on a well-executed plan.

The trip back to the licensing office was less eventful with Salim driving more cautiously.

Once in the parking lot, the two exited the vehicle and the officer said, "Salim, you are a fine driver, and I am happy to issue you a license. Congratulations."

Six years later, during a dinner celebrating his graduation with honors from a university in the United States, Salim asked to address the young Muslim students in attendance. When the room went silent, Salim pulled his driver's license from his wallet, and holding it out for all to see he said, "I'd like to tell you the story of the true Messiah who, when you ask him how to obtain a license from a corrupt government, will not only help you drive but also save a cat and cause you to love your enemy. Above all else, though, Jesus will call you into the true identity he has given you before the foundations of the world."

Where Does My Help Come From?

Let's return to the aspiring yet floundering future King David.

It's evident in 1 Samuel 30:1–6 that David and his mighty men are having a very bad day. Their town has been burned and their wives and children have been taken captive by the Amalekites. To add to David's distress, his men, "each one . . . bitter in spirit because of his sons and daughters," were talking of stoning him (v. 6 NIV).

I want to make an observation here that I think is instructive when we find ourselves in times of trauma and pain. Notice that both David and his men "lifted up their voices and wept until they had no more strength to weep" (v. 4). Though both David and his men wept, notice the different results of their crying out. David's men began discussing the idea of killing David, but David "encouraged and strengthened himself in the Lord his God" (v. 6).

In my opinion, this is an example of the difference between complaining and lamenting.

To complain (Hebrew, אָנַן—"to murmur; debate") results in negative outcomes because complaining is sourced in falsehood and deception. Typically, complaining is the result of a victim identity that is impatient and self-absorbed. Complaining ultimately leads to death. In Numbers 11:1 we see what God thinks of complainers: "Now the people complained about their hardships in the hearing of the Lord, and when he heard them his anger was aroused. Then fire from the Lord burned among them and consumed some of the outskirts of the camp" (NIV).

The result of David's men "weeping aloud" was a discussion of killing David—not a lot of the fruit of the Spirit in that plan.

Because our three sons were raised in very difficult living situations in the Muslim world, we had three guidelines for them to remember:

1. Honor all people (1 Pet. 2:17)—No disrespect. Ever.
2. Always speak truth (John 8:32)—No falsehood. Ever.
3. Give thanks in all things (1 Thess. 5:18)—No complaining. Ever.

We learned over time that no other guidelines were necessary.

To lament (Hebrew, סָפַד—"to mourn") results in comfort. "Blessed . . . are those who mourn [lament]," teaches Jesus in the Beatitudes, "for they shall be comforted!" (Matt. 5:4). Lament cries out in truth to truth himself.

I love the way Ann Voskamp, in her book *One Thousand Gifts*, summarizes the difference between lament and complaint: "Lament is a cry of belief in a good God, a God who has His ear to our hearts, a God who transfigures the ugly into beauty. Complaint is the bitter howl of unbelief in any benevolent God in this moment, a distrust in the love-beat of the Father's heart."[31]

Take a moment and ask God, "What do I do when I'm in pain? Holy Spirit, teach me to lament and not complain." The result of David's "weeping aloud" was encouragement and strength in the Lord his God.

Notice that just as quickly as David began his descent into the imposter shadow self by looking to himself for guidance,[32] he looked back up, out of himself, to God. In his poetry, David often emphasizes where our eyes should be focused. In a song of ascents, the psalmist (traditionally considered to be David) writes:

> I look up to the mountains and hills, longing for God's
> help.
> But then I realize that our true help and protection
> is only from the Lord,
> our Creator who made the heavens and the earth.
> He will guard and guide me, never letting me stumble
> or fall.

God is my keeper; he will never forget nor ignore me.
(Ps. 121:1–3 TPT)

You can give yourself the same reminder: *Why are you look-ing down here? Why are you looking at the ground? Why are you looking at other people? Look up! Up where Christ is seated above all. He's not under anybody. He's above all your enemies.* A down-and-out person is looking inward. A person filled with hope is looking up and out. Where are you looking today?

Scripturally speaking, true identity is received from God in community through the intuitive mind in prayer. The counter-feit of Christ-centered identity is radical individualism. Radical individualism is self-generated and subjective and leads only to internal and external conflict. Contrarily, true identity is the essence of who you are, gifted to you by God and meant to be discovered in relationship with him. It's the "I" you carry deep inside of you and secured in love, value, and worth. Your unique and true identity is meant to bless the world.

The kingdom of God is all about receiving from God. God will never give you the power to do something you aren't willing to do. I can pray all day long: "God, give me the courage to die for you. I'm not leaving the safety of my own neighborhood but help me to be courageous." But why would God answer that? Or "God, help me to trust you with money, but I'm not sacrificing any that I've worked so hard to earn." Why did you waste your breath praying that prayer? The prayers themselves are false.

But God is more than willing to strengthen and empower a mustard seed of faith. Yes, Lord, I believe, help me in my unbelief. When we come to the Lord in our true identity, we can accomplish more than we can ask or even imagine. It's unbelievable.

117

Stop the Traffic

I recently worked with a small group of law enforcement people at the federal level. They asked God, "Is there a new way to run a criminal task force that's never been done before?" Isn't that brilliant? You should see the ideas that have come to their minds. They are taking their true identity into their profession, laying it before God, and saying, "We are afraid that we will never be able to end human trafficking. We think you can end it, but we don't know how. Is there a way to run a task force to end human trafficking that has never been thought of before?"

Do you know what God's answer is to that question? Would God ever say, "Not that I know of"? If so, then why not just be an atheist? I would. It's more fun. It's less costly.

God's answer was, "Yes, there's a way to end human trafficking. There's a way to do it." With whom would God share this answer? People with the identity and intention to be in that work. Doesn't that make sense? I can pray, "God, give me the answer to human trafficking." But if I'm not in the trenches willing to do the work in my true identity, why would a solution be revealed to me? God did raise up a team of people to do just this. They've been rescued out of the pit by God and are living fearlessly in their true identity. The experiences in their lives have contributed to their despising human trafficking at every level. They're ready to do anything God tells them to do. And they are in a position to do it. They are meeting and putting together a strategy to eliminate human trafficking in one city. They're going to start with one city and go from there.

Do you want to be in a good community group? Be in one like that. Do you want to hear people pour their hearts out before God? Be in a group like that. It's not just talk. They know what they're doing with the Lord, and they're asking him to lead them—and he is. When you're in a group praying in your true identity, you'll see God move like you've never seen him move before. I could tell you stories like this from all over the world.

There are ways to do things about which we've never thought. Every medical professional knows there are cures we don't know yet for diseases. Every astronomer, every physicist knows there are things we don't know yet in the universe. We must figure them out. Why do we think we've figured out our relationship with the Lord? Understanding the depth of God is an eternal journey. We need to pursue it. Why? Because we've been made stewards of the mysteries of God![33]

Any Questions?

Back in 1 Samuel 30, when David and his men return home and find their families have been taken captive, we see that King David encourages and strengthens himself "in the LORD his God" (v. 6 NIV). As a result, circumstances begin to change. Avoiding a victim identity, David orders Abiathar the priest to bring him the ephod[34] with which David "inquired of the LORD" with two significant questions. First, "Shall I pursue this raiding party?" (v. 8 NIV). What kind of question is that? Wouldn't you automatically pursue the bad guys if they abducted your family? Maybe. But what's fresh in David's mind are the results of him making plans and decisions based on his own thoughts of self-promotion and self-protection. He is not willing to make that mistake again.

Second, David asks, "Will I overtake them?" (v. 8 NIV). What a great question. Why not ask the Lord about the completion of the task?

What is God's response to David's inquiry? "Too late, you blew it." No, it will never be. Where sin abounds, grace abounds much more.[35]

Don't you love the example of David throughout this situation? He met significant personal and professional failure with deep lament and turned his focus back on the Lord. Then, within the truth of who God made him to be, he sought wisdom from the God who speaks without reproach and condemnation.

Here are the two alternative strategies and their results:

1. David thought to himself = false identity, down to defeat.
2. David inquired of the Lord = true identity, up to victory.

The difference between these two strategies is dramatic. When we're in a situation, what should we do? We shouldn't say, "Lord God, do this and that for me . . ." Rather, we should ask, "God, what do you want me to know? What do you want me to do?"

That's inquiring of God, not telling God what to do. It's asking him for insight and direction. What God will tell you about knowing, you don't know yet. What God will tell you about doing, you won't have thought of yet. This is why we pray.

David, the man after God's own heart, experienced success when he first "inquired of the LORD." Nine times in the Bible David inquires of the Lord.[36] This feature is not seen in any other biography in the Old or New Testament.

As I have studied David's lines of inquiry, I think there are three main questions we should ask God before we move to action.

The first question is, *Should I go? Should I do this?*

We have lived in some very high-conflict areas. Our teams were made up of foreigners and nationals. Every day, our lives were on the line. In order to remain in the flow of God's generous grace for any situation and to access that place of perfect peace, we tried, and still try, to follow David's example with this same question: "God, should we go? Should we do this thing?"

Some of our team members have experienced unspeakable persecution. We don't just do seemingly brave things. We try to be diligent to first ask God, "Do you want me to talk to this person? Do you want me to go to that village? Do you want me to get in the car with those people?" Don't assume God wants you to talk to every single person you meet.

We are also following the example of Jesus. He doesn't want us to just imitate him. He is modeling for us how to know. He could hear from the Father and see what the Father was doing, so he knew what to do, where to go, who to talk to, who not to talk to, and when to walk away. He is modeling to us *how to know*.

The second question is, *Will I win?*

Is it okay to ask God if you're going to win? What do you think? Are you too shy to ask? I don't know if winning is important to you or what race you are running. I do know I want to win my race. I'm not saying winning means I achieve a certain thing. I just want to win. Do you think Jesus came to earth thinking, *I'm not sure if I want to win; that might be prideful.* He came to win. Peter didn't understand Jesus's way of winning; that's why he wanted Jesus to avoid the cross.[37]

Perhaps Peter was thinking something like this: "Jesus, I know you're committed to God and all, but I think the cross is a bad idea. I'm against the idea of our leader being killed. I'm not a big fan of persecution when persecution can be avoided by taking safer courses of action. Can't you just take out the bad guys and make our team win?"

Does Jesus say, "Wow, I love your heart, Peter. I love your compassion for suffering people"? No. Jesus turned to Peter and said, "Get out of my way, you Satan! You are a hindrance to me, because your thoughts are only filled with man's [fearful] viewpoints and not with the ways of God" (Matt. 16:23 TPT). Peter wanted Jesus to win by his own cultural standards. Jesus wanted to win according to God's good, perfect, and pleasing will.

I don't think we realize how often we say things without thinking or considering the ways of the kingdom of God. The truth Jesus is actually conveying is, "Peter if I don't die, you die. If I don't die, you all go to hell."

Someone once asked me a great question, and while we were talking about next steps, he made a certain statement which is a good example of the point I am making about Peter's wrong thinking.

The person I was talking with said, "I'm a loner." I stopped him. What kind of statement is *I'm a loner*? It is an identity statement. So I asked, "Did Jesus come to you and say you were a loner? Did Jesus make any loners?" No, he didn't. The statement was wrong. But how many of us would sit in tacit agreement and let it go in most Christian meetings? All the while, Satan is saying, "Ha ha, my lie is going throughout your group, and you don't even know it."

Being a loner kills people; it destroys their lives. It's an extremely damaging thing to think about ourselves. But we say, "Oh, you're a loner; that's okay," when it's not okay. Do you see how clever the enemy is? We believe perceived truth statements that are false. And we welcome them and even agree with them. God doesn't make loners. He creates us with the capacity for connection in communities. That's what he does. Communities are strong and powerful, and they're built on love relationships. In genuine community, everyone in their true and unique identity *belongs*. Loners self-destruct in isolated, dark places.

When David, in his true identity as shepherd-poet-warrior-king, inquired of the Lord, his questions were, "Should I go?" and "Will I win?"

My question to the Lord is, "When we do this, will it work?" I want to know that God's plan will work. I ask because I want his reassurance that his perfect love will cast out all my fear.

It's similar to when a kid asks their father, "Dad, if I jump into the pool, am I going to drown? You're telling me to do this, but is it going to work? Will I make it? If I start to struggle, will you help me?" Most dads will say, "Yes. Come on, it will work! I will be right here to help you. You are going to do it, and it will be fine!" That's how God communicates also.

The third question to ask before moving to action is, *How should I go?*

When you ask the questions Should I go? Will I win? and How should I go? your life with God will become generative and creative.

A friend in our community group was considering the idea of starting a winery. Do you think Jesus likes wineries? I think he does. Before making a decision, he spent time in prayer asking God these three questions: Should I do this? Will I be successful? How should I do it?

Asking that third question in this context is interesting because there is already an established formula for starting a winery. It's a set pattern, and this pattern is guarded by the hierarchy of winery people. You do not violate the pattern. Yet my friend's question to God was about the potential of discovering and developing a new way to start and run a winery. Is there a way to do it that's never been done before? That was his question.

He put a little group together, and they started praying about it. Eventually, they came up with a completely disruptive way to run a winery and tried it. Today, they have a very successful business that has been applauded in the winery culture for its innovation and success.

God is the Creator God, and his people, created in his image, are cocreators with him. If you sense God is calling you to do something, take the time to pray and meditate as you think about how you should do it. The same way as everybody else? What's a new way to think about it and implement it?

Scripture tells us that as we present ourselves to God as living sacrifices, holy and acceptable to him, we are to stop conforming our lives to the patterns of this world but be constantly transformed by the renewing of our minds.[38]

Remember the three big questions: Should I go? Will I win? How should I go?

Make the Big Ask

Let's pray and ask God about your true identity. When you sweep the house clean of false identities, Jesus said not to leave the house empty because if you do, the enemy will return with greater strength. We are going to be listening for the voice of God in our hearts through the Holy Spirit. This is not mindfulness or self-affirmation.

I prayed an identity prayer with a man who is the three-time president of one of the wealthiest companies in the United States. He is a follower of Jesus, and he has never thought about asking God questions and then listening for answers.

Before we prayed together, he said, "I just want you to know that my company hires experts in self-affirmation to counsel our employees. That's how we've made it as far as we have, why we make so much money. We're experts in self-actualization."

I said, "I'm not talking about self-affirmation or actualization."

Mindfulness and self-affirmation involve sweeping your house clean and trying to keep the enemy out by sheer willpower. It might work for a moment, but it isn't lasting transformation that sets a person free.

I asked the man, "How's your life going with self-affirmation?"

He said, "Well, I've made a lot of money, but my family has suffered in the process."

I said, "Let's try sweeping the house clean and letting Jesus step inside," and he agreed.

It has so transformed his life that he takes me with him to meetings and says, "This is my friend Jamie. Jamie, tell them what you do." And before I can start, he interrupts and says, "Never mind, just do it with them."

He wants every one of his friends and employees to know how to hear God's voice and live in their true Christ identity. He's committed to the process.

Understanding our own true identity gives us opportunity to walk others, often people of great influence, into understanding their own identities in Christ.

I'm going to ask the Lord to say what he calls you or how he refers to you or sees you—not just a moniker, but your identity. Whatever you sense, think, or hear, write it down immediately. Usually, it is the very first thing that comes to your mind.

You may ask, "Jamie, how will I know it's God speaking and not my own mind?" You will know it's God speaking because whatever it is you sense from the Holy Spirit will be encouraging, it will align with Scripture, and it won't involve accusation or condemnation. And, whatever you hear, think, or sense from the Holy Spirit should resonate with you.

Father, thank you for this reader. I bless them in the name of the Father, Son, and Holy Spirit.

Father, thank you that you are always with us. You never leave us. You never forsake us. Whether we want you here or not, you are here. You are omnipresent, and you love us. You never give up on us. You never just walk away from us out of frustration. You are always with us. You don't ever want us to be afraid. You want us to be filled with love and joy and peace and patience and the things of the Spirit. Lord, I know that you are moving among us. You are making us think through things we wouldn't normally think about.

Lord, we've been down in the trash pile. Now we want to lift our eyes up to you. We've looked at the false and we want to speak truth about it.

Lord, clean us out as we give these false identities to you. We give them to Christ. As Christ bears the false identities in his own flesh, he exchanges false identity for true identity. When we give him our shame, he gives us back honor. When we give him our guilt, he gives us back innocence. When we give him our fear, he gives us back power and authority. It's an exchange at the cross. That's why the cross is so beautiful to us. We can leave our burdens there, and you hand us back life. Father, as we have given you these false identities, and as we are safe within your protection and your silencing of the enemy and all the false things in our lives, in your beautiful voice, Lord, would you speak back to us the name or the identity that you call us? What do you say about us, Lord? What do you call us?

Quickly write down the first thing you hear, see, think, or sense from the Holy Spirit. If you don't hear anything, that's fine. We'll address that later. For now, write down your first impression, even if it doesn't make any sense to you.

How do you refer to us, Lord Jesus?

This is the way Jesus serves us. He calls us by name. The sheep hear his voice because he calls us by name. How does God refer to you? Even if it's hard to believe, just write it down.

Whenever the Lord says something to you, this is your answer back to him: Yes, I receive it. Thank you.

Now say out loud what you sensed from God about your identity.

It is important to consider how the enemy desires a foothold in this identity process. The enemy, Satan, has a strategy against you. His number one strategy is to blind you to the truth of your identity and destiny. That strategy is for you to live a mediocre life and die in false belief, having never known who you are or what you were created to be. That's his number one strategy.

However, when you step into the kingdom of God through embracing what Christ has done for you and you start to wonder why you are there and what your purpose is, you begin to ask identity questions. You will discover your identity. Or you will stumble onto a book like this about finding your true identity. Why? Because the enemy can never take your identity away from you. It's given to you by God, and no one can ever rob you of it.

His number one strategy, though, is that you're not aware of it or even wonder about it. The number two strategy of the enemy is that you discover your identity but he works to make you hate it. He works to make you dislike your identity in the kingdom of God.

For example, a gentleman I know gives his false identities to Jesus and then asks, "God, what do you call me?" He senses God saying, "You're my fixer." Fixer—like a repairer of things. Beautiful.

God will only call you a name he would call himself. That's another way you know it's from God. He names us after himself, like a good father does. He'll call you something that moves you forward in freedom. It's something that excites you, brings you joy and peace. Sometimes what God says about us is almost too beautiful to believe.

Being able to hear God is a new skill. It's like learning how to understand Morse code. You have to practice; it's a discipline. Or it's like tuning in to a radio frequency. You turn the knob but there are so many voices and so much static and noise. Then, finally, you find the station with the voice you recognize. The frequency resonates with your heart, and you keep fine-tuning it until the voice is crystal clear. You learn to hear God's voice above all other voices.

Hearing God's voice may be new to you. Maybe you hear God's voice but it's faint—a still small voice. The enemy, however, still lurks nearby with the old familiar voices.

Back to the gentleman who sensed God call him "fixer." Great, there's God speaking. Then, just as God speaks, another voice comes in. We quickly recognize this other voice because we've been listening to it our entire life, and we're experts at hearing not only the enemy's voice but also our own reasoning and analytical voice above God's.

This man hears "fixer." Then the thought comes to his mind that he'll be repairing things the rest of his life, and that idea makes him reject the identity of fixer. Isn't that brilliant? Hats off to Satan. He is deviously clever. Just as quickly as God says "fixer," Satan defines what "fixer" is and the man rejects the identity.

How do you know the difference between the two voices?

One is positive and one is negative. The term *fixer* in his mind is kind of neutral. He wonders, "What does 'fixer' mean?" And he feels some negative emotions.

Emotions come from God. Satan can't create emotion. He's not a creator. He can't create anything; he only imitates. Emotions were given to us by God. Emotions are a warning mechanism in our limbic system. Negative emotions warn us that something is wrong. Just like physical pain tells us something is physically wrong, emotional pain tells us something is emotionally wrong. Negative emotions tell us that what we believe is false. That's the value of negative emotions. Negative emotions are not our enemy.

Let's say I'm considering leaving my current job to risk making a career change. As I anticipate the future risk, I use my imagination. Most of us use our imagination to picture a worst-case scenario.

In the worst-case-scenario thinking, I take the new job, and it's a disaster. I fail. I get fired. I become homeless and my spouse leaves me because she didn't want me to take the risk in the first place.

My friend Paul Young calls this *future tripping*. In this type of thinking, my limbic warning system goes into action: fear, fear, fear. I feel fear because the scenario I'm playing out in my mind is false. FEAR = False Evidence Appearing Real. Fear wakes me up to danger. The negative emotion is an invitation from God to seek him and his truth about the situation.

So what do we do with negative emotions? We often try to bury them. We say, "I'm a Christian, I don't live by emotion. I live by facts." Untrue! Some say, "Faith is not a feeling." Mine is. Every situation in life affects our emotions.

Emotions, however, are not decision-makers. Emotions are the warning system. When my mind is fixed on things that are true, my emotions are love, joy, peace, patience, goodness, kindness, gentleness, faithfulness, and self-control. Even if the things I'm thinking about, such as suffering and persecution, might involve pain, I can still be at rest.

One of our national friends in a country where we formerly worked was detained and then tortured last year due to his vocal faith in Christ. The secret police would wrap him in plastic and then force him to stand in the sun where he would become dehydrated. In the evening, they would hang him up by his hands and cut him with razor blades. While cutting him, the police would order him to renounce Christ.

Our teammate reported that every time the police cut him, he could hear Jesus whispering in his ear, "I'm inside your pain. Every time they cut you more of me comes out."

Do you know what his emotions were in that situation? Joy. Peace. Because Christ appeared to him in the suffering, and his grace was abundant and generous for the place.

We read the amazing stories in the Bible about how people respond to persecution and we want them to be true, but we mostly don't believe them to be true. "Oh, yeah, they're singing in dungeons and praising God in coliseums? Yeah, right."

But true joy was flowing from our tortured teammate because his mind was fixed on truth. The prophet Isaiah writes, "Perfect, absolute peace surrounds those whose imaginations are consumed with you; they confidently trust in you" (Isa. 26:3 TPT).

Your mind is powerful. If you lay in bed at night and think about exercising, your mind will make your body prepare to exercise. That's its power. Your mind will believe the real and the unreal just as quickly, depending on what you want to focus on. Your imagination doesn't distinguish between real and unreal. If you fix your imagination on the things of God, you can be joyful no matter what's going on.

After cutting our teammate dozens of times, the police realized that the young man was finding joy within the torture. They said, "We've either got to kill him or let him go. The problem is, it seems like he wants us to kill him."

They arrived at this conclusion because our teammate kept calling out to Jesus that he wanted to see him face-to-face. In the pain, our friend felt deep joy, but the thought of seeing Jesus face-to-face brought tears to his eyes.

"What do I have to do to get you to move in front of me so I can see your face, Jesus?" he called out.

He sensed Jesus saying, "You'd have to come home with me."

What do you think our teammate said he wanted to do? He wanted to go. He was truly experiencing what Paul described: "To live is Christ and to die is gain" (Phil. 1:21 NIV).

What if you believed like that? You would be invincible and eternally at rest.

The secret police said, "If we kill him, it's going to be the greatest joy of his life. Let him go."

"No," our teammate cried out. "No."

So they released him.

He came back to us. He was twenty-five years old at the time, a young Muslim who had come to Christ and had been a believer for only one year when he was tortured. You show me a twenty-five-year-old American Christian who can do that. Yet people ask, "Is he a real believer?" Oh my gosh.

He was frustrated. He said, "I was so close to seeing Jesus. I was almost right there, and then they stopped." We were thinking, *God, we don't want to be that close. We're happy right here. We don't want to die.*

One year later, at age twenty-six, our young Muslim friend and follower of Jesus is participating in a late-night Bible study in the desert. He and his friends would travel out there at night to meet up with an American who drove a van filled with lawn chairs out into the desert to lead secret Bible study groups.

The American would set up a circle of chairs at a predetermined location and then wait for the Muslims to appear out of the night to study the Scriptures with him.

They would study the Bible through the night, and just before dawn they would pray, embrace, and then vanish back into the desert.

On this night, he is explaining a reoccurring dream he's been having. "I keep dreaming that I'm walking through my darkened house with a flashlight trying to locate my family, but I keep draping a cloth over the light, making it less visible. I think God is trying to tell me something, but I don't understand."

One of the other Muslim believers reads aloud Matthew 5:15–16: "And who would light a lamp and then hide it in an obscure place? Instead, it's placed where everyone in the house can benefit from its light. So don't hide your light! Let it shine brightly before others, so that your commendable works will shine as light upon them, and then they will give their praise to your Father in heaven" (TPT).

The young Muslim believer concludes, "Oh, I know what that means. I need to get my whole tribe [extended family] together and explain Jesus to them."

The following day, he goes to his uncle and says, "I need the whole tribe together so I can talk about how I've come to faith in Jesus."

His uncle warns him, "If I call the tribe together and you speak of these things, some may plan to kill you."

But the young Muslim believer is beyond the fear of death. It's not that he is brave; he is fearless.

Four hundred people come out, and he gives his testimony. Two days later, three cousins drag him out in the desert and shoot him between his legs to shame and castrate him. Then they leave him there to die.

But he doesn't die. He is found by some shepherds who take him to a small hospital. There, a doctor saves his life but informs him that he'll never have children and never walk again.

But his body heals, and he can have children, and he does walk again.

After his recovery, he goes back to his uncle and says, "Let's do it again. I need to speak to them again. Apparently, they didn't understand what I meant because they took it the wrong way."

When he informs us that he wants to go back and speak to his tribe again, we are horrified. We warn him not to do it. We, his "mature" disciplers! Do you know why we are afraid? Because we don't believe the gospel like he believes the gospel. We haven't experienced the tangible presence of Jesus as he has. That is where the Lord is challenging us.

The young Muslim goes back to his tribe and speaks to them again. The ones who shot him are right in the front row. He says, "Apparently you didn't understand my message. I forgive you in the same way that Jesus forgives you. It's okay. I'm fine." He then proceeds to explain the gospel again.

Two days later, the same guys abduct him, stab him multiple times, and push him down a ravine in a desert-like wilderness, thinking he will bleed out.

This time he is discovered by a military patrol doing night maneuvers. They pick him up and ask, "What happened to you?"

"My cousins stabbed me," he says.

"Why?" the soldiers ask.

"Because I met Jesus."

These Muslim soldiers are amazed at his story. When he tells them what happened the first time, they ask, "You spoke to your tribe again after they shot you?"

"Yes."

"Who is this Jesus you're talking about?"

The soldiers are so moved by his courage that they go and find the cousins and arrest them.

Let God handle the vengeance part; you just forgive.

How is this young Muslim believer so fearless? He would say it's because he knows the God who speaks, and he knows his identity in the kingdom of God.

In our earlier example, a gentleman gives his false identities to Jesus and then asks, "God, what do you call me?" He hears "fixer." And right away, the temptation is to believe the enemy who says, "You're just going to be a fixer of things the rest of your life." He rejects the identity of fixer because he interprets what he thinks it means. He hears it and jumps to conclusions in his own knowledge, as his own source of what he thinks is real.

But there is a better way. Stay in the flow of God's communication. Don't start analyzing it and trying to figure it out. Ask God, "How do you define the identity of Fixer? I want your interpretation of that name, not the enemy's definition." And when this man heard the interpretation from God, it was beautiful and joy producing. "It's Hebrews 12:2," he told me later. "I help people *fix* their eyes on Jesus. I'm the fixer."

Who is defining the words in your life for you?

When God calls you something, don't go to the enemy to ask what it means, which you do by analyzing and jumping into future scenarios that you don't have grace for. Then fear kicks in and you begin to hate it, and you'll reject the very thing God is trying to offer you by letting the enemy be the interpreter of what God says. Be careful of this. Don't analyze and become introspective, just receive and continue to ask, "God, what else do you want me to know?" And write it down. Then ask, "God, when you see me in this identity, what do I look like to you?" Always write down what you sense and share it with a trusted friend or small group.

I promised you earlier that we'd explore the question, What if I didn't hear anything? There are typically two reasons why people don't hear or sense anything at all during the prayer exercises.

One reason is forgiveness. If there is any place in your life where you are unable or unwilling to receive God's forgiveness, how can he talk to you about anything else? God desires first and foremost that you know, live, and experience his absolute grace and forgiveness. Forgiveness is the oxygen you breathe in the kingdom of God.

Scripture teaches the following:

This is how much God loved the world: He gave his Son, his one and only Son. And this is why: so that no one need be destroyed; by believing in him, anyone can have a whole and lasting life. God didn't go to all the trouble of sending his Son merely to point an accusing finger, telling the world how bad it was. He came to help, to put the world right again. (John 3:16–17 MSG)

Throughout the coming ages we will be the visible display of the infinite riches of his grace and kindness, which was showered upon us in Jesus Christ. For by grace you have been saved by faith. Nothing you did could ever earn this salvation, for it was the love gift from God that brought us to Christ! So no one will ever be able to boast, for salvation is never a reward for good works or human striving. (Eph. 2:7–9 TPT)

If you do not live within God's forgiveness, most likely the Lord will want to speak to this issue first in your life.

Forgiveness is like a coin; it has two sides. The first side is about you. Ask the Lord, "Is there any place in my life where I believe I am unable to experience your forgiveness?" Let the Holy Spirit reveal this area to you and then lead you through a process of release and restoration.

The flip side of the coin is about others, the refusal to forgive another person. If you come to the Lord and want to talk to him but you refuse to release another person in forgiveness, he's not going to talk to you about anything else except releasing that person or persons in forgiveness. We think he is silent, but we just aren't listening to the foundational piece that opens up the flow of communication. Unforgiveness is like a kink in a hose that blocks movement.

Time and again, Scripture warns us about the absolute necessity of forgiving others. Jesus says, "If you are offering your gift at the altar and there remember that your brother or sister has something against you, leave your gift there in front of the altar. First go and be reconciled to them; then come and offer your gift" (Matt. 5:23–24 NIV).

Is there someone with whom you are angry and unforgiving? If there is, your unforgiveness keeps you connected to that other person in a form of spiritual bondage.

For victims of any kind of abuse, forgiveness is critical. We train police officers in this issue so that when they're dealing with victims, they can help the victims release the abuser in forgiveness. This is not to excuse the abuser, who deserves the full legal consequences of their unlawfulness, but in order that the victim can move into a place of healing and restoration as quickly as possible. This is done in a very professional way, and it can help release the victim from years of PTSD because the officer on the scene is teaching the victim how to cut the offender off in forgiveness.

Can you imagine policing like that? Serving and protecting as opposed to law enforcing.

We worked with a police officer who was overly aggressive on the job, and as part of a disciplinary action, he was referred to our team. Like most people, his aggression was rooted in fear. We dealt with his fear and then watched him interact with the public. Prior to our training, he would pull over a vehicle and start accusing the driver of violating various traffic codes. After our training, the traffic stop sounded like this:

Officer: "You're driving eighty in a fifty-five zone. Are you okay? Are you anxious about anything? What are you afraid of in your life that is causing you to drive like this?"

Driver: "What?"

Officer: "I'm concerned that you're going to hurt yourself or someone else. What's going on inside of you that's causing you to drive like this? Are you anxious? What are you worried about? What's the matter? How can I help you?"

You know what drivers do in this scenario? They confess. They truth tell. As a police officer, people I pulled over for traffic offenses told me all kinds of things about their lives. People are lonely. People need places to confess, to tell the truth about their fear, guilt, and shame. Why wouldn't we teach this to the people we pay to serve and protect us? We need police officers who love people.

Some people ask, "So what do you do, stop writing tickets?" Oh no. There are people who don't want to be served and protected. They get the ticket. But people who do want to be served and protected, we serve and protect them.

Issues of forgiveness and unforgiveness are a first significant block to hearing God. The second reason people don't hear or sense God speaking during the prayer exercises has to do with anger. If you're mad at somebody, your anger has to be resolved before you can receive anything from the Lord. You can't hear God through anger. It's attached to unforgiveness.

Anger and unforgiveness are the two big blocks to hearing God. If I'm praying with a person and they respond with, "Nothing, nothing. I can't hear or sense anything," I encourage them to relax, and then I ask, "Is there any place in your life where you feel unforgiven by God? Is there any place in your life where you refuse to forgive another person? Are you angry with someone?"

When the issue is revealed, we take it to Jesus. The Lord wants to free the person of these issues. Once they're free of these, they can seek God on other issues.

Hearing communication from God should be a normal, everyday occurrence. It takes practice and intentionality. It's not magic. And please remember, if I can do this with a hostile person in the Middle East, then you can do this anywhere!

Listening to God produces internal peace that results in external peace. Paying attention, being aware, and receiving the annunciations of divine love and truth resolve conflict in your inner world and then overflow to the people of the world. You can't give away what you don't have. Let's agree to stop reacting in fear, guilt, and shame and begin exchanging our reality for God's truth so that we can effortlessly and fearlessly give away the peace that we receive.

PART 4

ACTION

Vision without action is merely a dream.
Action without vision just passes the time.
Vision with action can change the world.

JOEL A. BARKER

Act on what you hear!

JAMES 1:22 MSG

If you are abiding by God, paying attention, being aware, and responding to his annunciations, you will engage in meaningful and transformative actions.

According to biblical scholars, David is between ten and fifteen years old when he is anointed king of Israel by the prophet Samuel.[1] First Samuel 16:13 states that "Samuel took the horn of oil and anointed him in the midst of his brothers. And the Spirit of the LORD *rushed upon David from that day forward*" (ESV, emphasis added).

Imagine yourself as a ten-year-old filled with the Holy Spirit and understanding your identity from God in Christ. Children today are getting their identity from friends and social media because parents are getting their identity from what they do, what they have, and what people think of them. It is no wonder that our nation is struggling with such internal and external conflict. We as a nation have lost our sense of identity and destiny.

At about age seventeen (a junior in high school), filled with God's Spirit and settled in his sense of true identity, David encounters the national threat of the Philistines and their champion, Goliath. David is young and confident, and he wants to take on the challenge that is filling his fellow countrymen with fear and shame.

When we are young, God is building into us identity. You don't have to be a Christian; it's what God does for all people because God knit together each of us in our mother's womb. God built identity into each of us. God wants us to understand our identity, but the enemy, the world, and the flesh work to crush it out of us. That's the way this fallen world works—replacing truth with falsehood.

As a kid out in the fields, David learns to be a shepherd. He learns to write poetry, and he learns to fight the lion and the bear with a sling. His heart comes alive when he is engaged in these activities because, with God's help, David is becoming his true self.

As a result, when he comes on the scene with Goliath, he's ready to engage. He doesn't even ask God what to do. He recognizes the situation, and he knows what to do.

How does the enemy challenge young David to try to keep him from figuring out that he's invincible when walking with God in his identity? Remember, the enemy attacks identity!

The first challenge to David's sense of identity comes from *the people in his own family*. His brothers accuse him of being arrogant and remind him that he is nothing but a lowly, insignificant shepherd: "Now Eliab his eldest brother heard what he said to the men; and Eliab's anger was kindled against David and he said, Why did you come here? With whom have you left those few sheep in the wilderness? I know your presumption and evilness of heart; for you came down that you might see the battle" (1 Sam. 17:28).

These are some serious accusations from his big brother. David's older brothers are the soldiers. They're the ones at the battlefront, but they accuse him of being arrogant. Why? What is David doing that is so presumptuous and evil? Perhaps Eliab was already angry. Here's baby brother (who was anointed in front of them, no less) unarmed, standing there on the battle line with the "real men." And he is questioning them: "What's in it for the man who kills that Philistine and gets rid of this ugly blot on Israel's honor? Who does he think he is, anyway, this uncircumcised Philistine, taunting the armies of [the Living God]?" (v. 26 MSG).

People hate when you ask these kinds of questions because then they have to confess. They are forced to face the truth: they are afraid.

Yes, we are afraid to speak out our inner truth.

David's brother doesn't want to be afraid, so he projects hostility onto the person asking the question. This is what fearful people do—blame others for their fear.

If we walk into a situation in our true identity, and we're paying attention to God, aware of what's happening, and can hear what God says and know what to do, people may become jealous because they're fearful and fear produces shame.

When you endeavor to live out your true identity, the identity that you hear God call you, you will face opposition. The opposition may even come from your own family, from your own team. Jesus experienced this himself.

Like Jesus, David doesn't receive the cursing judgment of others. With wisdom beyond his young years, he recognizes that these curses are from his brother's false identity rooted in fear and insecurity. He simply rejects the false identity and continues to move in the truth of who he is. He forgives his brother and moves forward with his life.

If I teach a class or deliver a lecture and someone comes up to me afterward and says, "You're the worst speaker I've ever heard in my life," I simply don't receive it. Why would I? I go to God and ask, "Lord, what did you think? What do you want me to know? What do you want me to do?" I intentionally and consistently engage with God to listen for his interpretation of the events of my life.

Believe me, God is a good critic, and he's thorough. God talks about even the thoughts and intentions of my heart when I'm speaking, not just about my timing and delivery. He talks about that too, but more about my heart. Why would I receive hostile critique from an angry person when I have the edifying, constructive critique of the Holy Spirit available to me?

Do you know why a person would endure a scenario such as that? Because the person lacks any sense of their own true self. Do you know why little kids get bullied? They have no sense of true identity, so they allow others to name them.

A person with an identity cannot be bullied. They can be beaten up and even killed, but they can't be bullied because they're not afraid. Kids are bullied because they have no identity, and they're getting their identity from the bully. That's chronic in America because America doesn't have any identity.

What starts in the heart works out into the culture. A parent with no identity cannot give a kid identity. A teacher with no identity cannot teach a class about identity in a public or a Christian school. The type of school doesn't matter. What matters is whether the teacher has a sense of identity.

David rejects the false accusation of his family. I'm not proud. It's not because I'm arrogant. I know the situation. I recognize it, and I'm going to do something about it.

The second challenge to David's sense of identity comes from *his own leadership*. King Saul says to David, "You can't go and fight this Philistine. You're too young and inexperienced— and he's been at this fighting business since before you were born" (v. 33 MSG).

Again, David simply refuses to accept the incorrect assessment. He informs Saul that he has practiced fighting bears and lions, and this Philistine will fare no better. The Lord will rescue him.

Saul assumes David will go to battle as soldiers always do. His army hasn't thought of any new ways to fight, so they can't adjust to the new tactics of the enemy. David has learned a new way to fight and knows he will not lose if he fights in his own identity.

What does Saul do? "Then Saul outfitted David as a soldier in armor. He put his bronze helmet on his head and belted his sword on him over the armor" (vv. 38–39 MSG).

Why would you keep doing the same thing over and over again if it doesn't work? Perhaps the strategy worked once, but it has lost its effectiveness. Why continue in compulsive repetition? That's the definition of insanity. Why would we do that? Why do we do it with God?

If the routine you have with God has not worked, why would you work at it harder or more often? Is God an animistic tribal deity that if you perform the rituals and formulas often enough, he'll finally respond to you? Who wants that god? I don't.

I want the God who initiates life and relationship with me even when I'm not asking. I want the God who loved me even when I was his enemy. I want the God who says to David, "Hey, let me teach you how to fight in a new way, because one day, about ten years from now, you're going to really need it. You don't know it yet, you're not going to trust me yet, but you will. Trust me now in the small, seemingly unimportant things.

Learn to do what I say. Throw a rock at that lion. Do it. Trust me, because one day it's going to make you king. You can do this, trust me."

Is that how we teach our young kids? Do we teach them to experience every day like that? To trust the voice of God like that?

King Saul says David has to fight Goliath like his soldiers do. But David tries on the old armor and says, "I cannot go with these, because I am not used to them" (v. 39 AMP). And he removes Saul's armor. Then David takes his shepherd's staff, selects five smooth stones from a brook and puts them in the pocket of his shepherd's pack, and with his sling in hand approaches Goliath.

David doesn't receive the false identity based on the lie that he has to fight like everybody else. David knows the way to victory is to fight in the true identity he received from God.

Family can be an obstacle. Leadership can be an obstacle. The third challenge to David's sense of identity comes from *the enemy himself.*

Goliath has to get David to come to him. He has to or he's not going to win. So how can he get David to come out of his identity and fight in Goliath's identity? That's Goliath's only chance.

Goliath's thinking must have been something like this: *I can't chase this kid around, and if he's good with those rocks, even if they don't kill me, they're going to hurt like crazy all day long because I'm never going to catch him. I've got to get him to come to me and fight my way. Then I will beat him.*

This is how Satan works in everyday life. He thinks, *I have to get this person to come to me in a wrong identity. I've got to get them to come to me and fight the way I want to fight so that they will lose.*

We fall for this strategy all the time. Someone cuts us off in traffic and the enemy is right there saying, "That person disrespected you! What are you going to do about it?" And that's all it takes.

Suddenly all that unworthiness and shame comes boiling out. "I'm going to make that person respect me! I'm going to make them see me!"

Why?

"Because nobody's ever respected me in my whole life."

Who didn't respect you?

"My dad didn't respect me. My brother didn't respect me."

Wow! How long have you been driving around with that lie going on inside of you? That's what kills us—false identity.

We're learning to remember that in every situation we have a choice about how we'll respond. We can say, "Wait a second. Why am I so mad about this?" Instead of fuming and raging, we can ask God, "Where is this hostility coming from? What's the source of it? Where did this first begin in my life? Search me, Lord. How does this situation make me feel? What do you want me to know about this, Lord?"

Once when I was on a business trip, my wife called me at my hotel. She woke me up to ask, "Are you eating dinner with a guy named Carl tomorrow night?"

I said, "Yes."

She said, "Do you know that you have a dinner scheduled with some other guy named Michael the same evening?"

I said, "Yes, I know this. I'm meeting Carl and Michael together." And I thought, *You called and woke me up to tell me there's a conflict in my calendar?* It made me frustrated, but before I said anything, I asked God, "What am I frustrated about? What's her motivation? She's trying to help me. Why am I upset? I'm upset because she woke me up and inconvenienced me."

If I pray and ask God, "Please wake me up at night to talk to me," would God say, "I don't want to inconvenience you. You get mad when your wife does it. Why would I do it?"

Do you see the disconnect? How could I ask God to wake me in the night watches and give me ideas about my life and future when I don't even want my wife to wake me up at night? I don't want anyone to wake me up at night. This is confession.

So I ask God, "What is this? I think I'm more important than what my wife thinks I am. I think I'm more valuable. Why do I want to defend that false self? Why do I have to protect that?"

I want to speak from my true identity. I am a militant peacemaker. I make peace with her. I don't want to go out of my identity in this little conflict because once I take that step, off we go.

I read an article about how raccoons fight dogs much larger and more powerful than them. The raccoon will lure the overly aggressive dog into a body of water and then drown the dog. Once the dog jumps into the water, all of its power is gone. The raccoon now owns the fight. That's a David and Goliath story.

Satan says to us, "Those people don't respect you. Go get them. God isn't going to do it, so you have to." This is the mistake Moses made.

Delivering a Deliverer

Moses was never afraid of Pharaoh, not one day. His parents were never afraid of Pharaoh. The writer of Hebrews tells us, "By faith Moses, after his birth, was hidden for three months by his parents, because they saw he was a beautiful and divinely favored child; and they were not afraid of the king's (Pharaoh's) decree" (11:23 AMP). Neither were the midwives afraid of Pharaoh. Scripture says these courageous women feared God more than Pharaoh.[2] Is it not reasonable to think Moses grew up realizing that although many of his Hebrew neighbors were terrified by the threats from Pharoah, there were those who knew God was more powerful.

That's how he was raised. Everyone Moses knew who defied Pharaoh, God prospered. The midwives were rewarded by God as were Moses and his parents. Instead of seeing their son murdered, Moses's parents watched their son grow up in wealth and power, without forgetting the truth of his identity.[3] God wants Moses to be unafraid of the threats of the world so that he can be trained by the very enemy he's going to go up against.

God is not afraid of the power of Egypt. God used Egypt to train Moses. Why not be trained by the most powerful nation in the world in order to raise up a new and greater nation? That makes perfect sense.

Moses understood the need to maintain his true identity. He saw himself as a Hebrew and a deliverer of his oppressed people. He holds on to his identity just as Daniel, Hananiah, Mishael, and Azariah will.[4]

These four famous friends rejected the identity of the Babylonians. They were Hebrews who would run Babylon. They did not view themselves as victims or captives. Instead, they determined to own the place in a short amount of time and become greater experts in Babylonian culture than the Babylonians themselves. How old were Daniel, Hananiah, Mishael, and Azariah? Twelve, thirteen? What were their parents like? Many exceptional youths were taken captive,[5] but these four stood out. Incredible.

Moses was walking among his people one evening when he saw an Egyptian taskmaster beating up a Hebrew. His true identity screamed out at the injustice. Imagine Moses's spiritual struggle in trying to decide how to respond.

On the one hand, his true self might have been encouraging him to seek God's wisdom and perhaps show restraint until the larger, national battle could be engaged.

On the other hand, his false self might have been encouraging him to allow his anger to be the decision-maker, whereby he could prove himself as a champion to the Hebrew people.

I feel certain the enemy was like the raccoon, luring Moses to jump into a battle where he has to forsake the strength of his position in Egypt.

Moses takes the bait and kills the Egyptian taskmaster, and for the first time in his life, Moses becomes afraid of Pharaoh. He also exchanges his true identity as a deliverer of oppressed people for that of a murdering exile. Moses is effectively banished from leadership for forty years because his ego got the better of him.

That's how the enemy works, tempting us to act in anger or fear without seeking wisdom from God. The enemy lures us into acting in our own wisdom and strength. Then when everything falls apart, he is there to accuse and shame us. At this point, we're susceptible to taking on a false identity. The enemy whispers, "Do you know who you are? I'll tell you who you are. You're nothing. Remember that. I know what you do when you think no one is watching." This is how the enemy talks all the time.

We all know this accusatory voice. We've all heard it at some point in our life. Funny, how easy it is to hear the enemy but how difficult to hear the Lord.

But here is how to respond when the enemy accuses: "God, I reject that in the name of Jesus. Who do *you* say that I am? I receive who you say that I am, and I say it out loud before all the heavenly realms. I receive your words of life to me."

In that hotel room when my wife awakened me with her phone call, I said, "Donna, let me put you on hold for a second." Then I said out loud, "I am a militant peacemaker. I will not engage in this dispute being provoked by the enemy!" My wife wasn't doing anything malicious; she was trying to help. Then I returned to Donna and said, "Thanks for checking on my schedule. I know the small details aren't my strong point. I so appreciate you keeping track of things for me. I love you. Good night."

These small battles are significant. Don't minimize them; they are important. The enemy knows you don't see them that way. Pay attention to what he's doing. Ask God, "What do you want me to know? What do you want me to do?" Especially when negative emotions come up, indicating that what you believe in the situation is wrong, ask God, "What is this? What is the source of this negative emotion? Where does it come from? Why do I feel unworthy and fearful in this situation? Help me to know myself."

In this way, you'll start to hear the Lord more clearly and consistently. You know why? Because you have the mind of Christ. Do you know the distance between your mind and God's mind? Zero. There is no distance. Jesus said it would be better for us if he left so that he could send the Holy Spirit to dwell in our hearts.[6]

God never stops communicating with us—never. If we go outside and the sunrise or the mountains cause us to say, "Wow," that is God. Every part of us that is moved by beauty and truth is God speaking within us. We sometimes miss the beauty and truth of the kingdom of God that surrounds us. We think if we're not actively participating in some cause for God that God isn't around.

An Unorthodox Orthodoxy

My Eastern Orthodox friends, when they're frustrated with us, call us crusaders. "You guys are always on a crusade against something." I think they may be correct. I'm an American Christian, therefore, I need a crusade. We can't just relax and abide in Christ. We have to get into the Middle East and convert those Muslims to Christianity. That's our job.

My Orthodox friends don't understand that kind of language because they've never been on a crusade. They weren't in the Crusades of the Middle Ages. They lived alongside the

Muslims and led them to Christ. They didn't want to conquer them.

When my Orthodox friends say something is the kingdom of God, they are usually referring to something of beauty and truth. One of them, a pastor in Jordan, said to me one time, "You know, Jamie, I was in the gas station the other day when the high priest of the Druze people approached me. He said that because of our relationship, he has begun to ask Jesus to speak to him. Isn't that so very kingdom of God?"

First of all, nobody gets access to the high priest of the Druze. Nobody. They are a very secretive group. It's astounding that this humble pastor has such incredible access. Second, the Druze do not acknowledge Jesus as the Christ of God. So this statement from the high priest was astounding.

I responded with, "That's awesome. You're going to win him?"

My Orthodox friend said, "No, no, this is kingdom. It's the kingdom moving. Relationship is not a cause or a crusade. It's the kingdom of God moving in all of its beauty. See that flower? That flower is also the kingdom of God in motion." He talked about a flower in the same way that he talked about the Druze man coming to Christ.

Isn't that kingdom? That's how Jesus talks. What are we trying to do? We're trying to move into the kingdom and move the kingdom forward. Isn't that beautiful? Lord, speak to me today.

Here's an exercise to practice: when you're stuck in traffic or somewhere else, just say, "Lord, remind me of a time when I was a child and you were communicating your love to me, and I didn't even realize it. Remind me of a time in my past when you were speaking to me, and I didn't know it was you."

You'll be surprised at the memories that come to your mind. It's really beautiful. You'll say, "Lord, that was you? I thought that was me talking to myself. That was you? When

I was setting up those little army men and making up stories? That was you talking to me about how we're going to do that together someday? That was you?" The Lord responds with something like this: "Why do you think it was so much fun? Because we were doing it together, just you and me. I made you to love that stuff."

God was there the whole time. Do you ever stop and think about that? He's been with you the entire time. Once you start to realize this, you live at another level of knowing.

In your mind, time will change. The past becomes something that serves to move you forward. The past doesn't chain you up and condemn you anymore. It moves you forward. I'm no longer afraid of past memories. I find God there with me, even in the difficult times.

I struggled with alcohol for much of my teen years and early adulthood. I can remember quite clearly taking my first serious drink at age fifteen and finding an immediate sense of relief from the anxiety I was dealing with in those years of my life. As alcohol became more and more my go-to coping mechanism, I began to engage in actions that would later plague my life. The consequences of my actions were real and needed to be addressed, but they did not need to carry with them an identity of shame. Dr. Brené Brown defines shame as "the intensely painful feeling or experience of believing that we are flawed and therefore unworthy of love and belonging."[7]

Therefore, the truth of Christ taking away my shame on the cross is indescribably liberating.[8] God's loving question to me wasn't what or how much I drank, but why? What lie that I believed about myself or God or others was I medicating with alcohol? God wanted to heal me and remove the false belief that was hurting me so deeply.

I learned that freedom and healing come in confession, in telling God the truth of what you feel deep inside of you: "Lord, this is how I feel right now. I feel angry. I feel ashamed. I feel hurt. Help me to know where in my past this comes from. What is this?"

Repentance is asking God to tell you his truth about the situation, his interpretation of a difficult memory when negative beliefs about yourself and life first formed. The memory remains the memory and part of the history of your life. But remembering with Jesus can change everything. He was there and wants you to know his perspective. This is revelation, and revelation always precedes transformation. And then you will know how to move to action.

First come attention, awareness, and annunciation, and then I can start doing what he says—action. This is what Jesus modeled. How did Jesus know to do and say the things he did? He could hear and see the Father.

How do we come up with new ideas about politics, religion, education, art, physics, culture, foreign policy, immigration, and so on? We have the mind of Christ and the Spirit of the living God dwelling in us. We have this great inheritance.

The difference between the ideas that come from God and those from someone who's just really good at coming up with them is that God's ideas transform the people involved. The ideas and resulting actions are redemptive.

Action begins in small steps. David learned by doing. As a young boy he learned to watch sheep, write poetry, and throw stones at enemies. These are the practices of a person whose identity is shepherd-poet-warrior-king.

Then one day, moving within his identity and vocation, he arrived at the battlefield. He saw the situation and recognized the scenario. His spirit jumped: "Wow, this is me! This is what God created me for." He moved quickly to step into the situation. The entire world screamed, "No, that's dumb. That's stupid. That's risky. Don't do that. You will fail."

Calculating and without drama, at age seventeen, David analyzed the current challenge of Goliath and weighed it against his training in smaller, less risky scenarios. He decided he was prepared and ran to the battle. Did you catch that, *he ran*! He defeated the giant Goliath in a matter of minutes.

Because of his courage and faith in who he is and who God is, David finally becomes king at age thirty.

At age fifty-one, however, David abandons his true identity to sit at home and play video games on the roof of his house. He is a shepherd-poet-warrior-king, but when he's not operating in his true identity, he's lazy, isolated, and powerless. In this frame of mind, he sees Bathsheba and down he goes.[9] That's how fast the enemy can get you. David is out of commission for two years. That's why walking and talking with the Lord every day is so important. "God, what do you call me? Say it again. I want to hear you say it again." And when you doubt, "Lord, what do you call me? You do not call me this. What do you call me?"

Let him speak to you and then you'll know what to do in your true identity; you'll know the action steps you need to take. Remember: attention, awareness, annunciation, and then action.

If we do all this listening and identity work but we don't put it into practice come Monday morning, it's a waste of our time. So before we reach the end of our journey together, let's develop some action steps. We're going to ask the Lord, "In relation to my identity, what do you want me to know and what do you want me to do?"

In the book of Acts when people receive the gift of the Holy Spirit, they go into immediate action. They don't just run around in circles; they know exactly where to go and with whom to speak. They also know how to speak the language of their focus people. They do what is unique to each one of them as determined by God.

That's what happens when you are aligned with the Spirit. The Spirit activates in you your unique identity and gifts. That's why the apostle Paul warns us never to quench or grieve the Spirit. You quench the Spirit by not listening. Fear, guilt, and shame quench the Spirit. Fear, in particular, is the great mind killer.

When God tells you to do something and you become fearful, the frontal parts of your brain shut down. The fight-flight-or-freeze response kicks in, and you become completely irrational. All you can do is try to protect yourself. Fear kills us, which may be why the number one exhortation from God in all of Scripture is "Do not be afraid."

We can learn to move through the fear rather than ignore it or merely cope with it. God will walk you through your fears gradually until you become courageous at very high levels of risk.

Let's dive in and pray!

Father, thank you for this reader. I bless them in the name of the Father, Son, and Holy Spirit.

Father, thank you for your willingness to communicate with us, for your willingness to talk with us, to live within us, to move us with your Spirit. Thank you for that. Lord, we've been thinking about false identity and getting rid of false identity. We've also prayed to hear from you about our true identity, and, Lord, it has activated thoughts and ideas within us. So, Father, we ask in the name of Jesus, would you say to each of us right now one thing you want us to do tomorrow to act in our true identity? One thing you want us to do in relation to our true identity? What is it, Lord?

Whatever it is you sensed from the Lord, write it down and do it. Remember, obedience is better than sacrifice. Be committed to talk to whomever you're supposed to talk to or go wherever you're supposed to go—whatever it is you sensed from the Lord. Just do it!

Another important action to take is to study whatever you sensed in prayer from the Lord about your identity. Find it in the Bible and research the use and meaning of the word, term, or phrase. Get in the Word first and find out everything you can about the identity you sensed. Study it there, and then go outside of the Bible and read on that topic. Study, learn, and grow.

Each day, as you're growing and learning, keep asking the Lord these questions: "What do you want me to know today to live into my true identity? And what do you want me to do?" Your *being*, your true self, will always inform your *doing*.

Remember that as the people in Acts start living their lives under the direction of the Spirit of God, it's an experiment. They have never experienced anything like this before. There are no books to read on the topic except the Torah. Everything is new to them.

For example, the Gentiles seem to be coming into the kingdom of God apart from the traditions of Judaism. What does that mean? They go back to the Old Testament and they have these debates and figure it out because they're experimenting.

You, too, are experimenting. "God, this happened today. What do you want me to know about this? What do you want me to do?" Or even while it's happening, ask, "What do you want me to know about this? What do you want me to do?" This is especially effective if you listen to God in community with other like-minded people.

The Fatality of Fear

We were teaching a class in Baghdad, Iraq, in 2003. It was a very tense time. We were living in central Baghdad with no military protection. Working in proximity with the US military made you a target. One part of our team was in another city and was ambushed and killed. I had to go to identify the bodies with the FBI and then come back to tell the rest of our team, most of whom were young singles or newly married and right out of college.

I came back from identifying the bodies and said to the young people, "Here are the facts as I understand them. Four people are dead. One survived. The survivor was shot multiple times, is in a coma, and has been medevacked to Germany. Their time has come to a finish. Now we have to talk about you all."

The young people were all believers, so I said to them, "You have to make a decision on what God wants you to do, knowing the risks of living here. What does God want you to know, and what does he want you to do? That's the question."

How do they know what action to take? Whether in war-torn chaos or comfortable in the United States trying to make a career choice, the question is the same: "God, what do you want me to know and what do you want me to do?" It's very straightforward and as undramatic as we can make it.

I warned them, "The danger for you is that you'll make a fear-based decision. Once you make a fear-based decision, you'll act in fear the rest of your life. Don't do that. Face the fear. Confess the fear. Move through the fear with God so the fear doesn't own you but you have authority over it in perfect peace. Do this before you ask what to do. Otherwise, you won't think with your whole mind; you'll only think out of the fear."

We inquired of the Lord starting with, "Lord, what do you want us to know about our fear?"

What do you think these young people were most afraid of? Dying, right? They were afraid of dying. We all are, aren't we? And if we're afraid to die, it says something about what we believe about God, doesn't it? God is either unable or unwilling to protect us at all times. The death of our teammates was evidence that God cannot or will not protect our people in Iraq. They're in coffins. There's the evidence.

The question, however, is not, What are the facts? The question is, What does God want me to know about these facts as they stand? We don't live in a dream world; it's a real world. These are real events that happened. "God, what do you say to me about this?"

God spoke to each one of them. I didn't tell them what I thought God would or should say. I just said don't make a fear-based decision because one fear-based decision leads to another, and to another, and for the rest of your life, you'll make decisions based in fear. It's a cycle that is hard to reverse.

Fear is an interesting thing. It is said that a crisis doesn't make a person; a crisis reveals a person. People who struggle with PTSD often aren't struggling only because of something that happened to them on the battlefield; they are struggling with something that was already present within them that the battlefield exposed. It's already present in them; it's just exacerbated in a crisis.[10]

The fear that these young people were dealing with in this situation was not from this situation. They brought the fear with them.

Each of them asked God, "What do you want me to know about fear?" God communicated to them about their individual fears, and we worked through them together.

And then they asked God, "What do you want me to do?" Each of the young people had the same sense about what God wanted. God said the same thing to each one: *Stay. I want you to stay. Staying here will be the best thing that's ever happened to you; leaving will be the worst mistake you could ever make.*

All of them stayed. They're in their midthirties now and married with families. Two of the couples are still in the Middle East today, and they are some of the most phenomenal people I know. They are fearless.

Here is our simple question to God right now: "God, what do you want me to know and what do you want me to do based on my identity?" After you do what you sense from him, you just keep asking, "And now what? What do you want me to do now?" Continue moving in your identity, and it will grow. God will start saying things to you that are more and more profound and life changing. This is faith. It's taking risks. This is transformation. It's acting on what you believe to be true.

Watch Jesus with the disciples. Like the disciples, you will stumble and you will fall and Jesus will pick you back up and you will keep going with him. The only danger is if you quit.

Kairos versus Chronos

This brings me to something I want to share about our concept of time.

In Scripture there are two kinds of time: *chronos* and *kairos*. Chronos time refers to minutes and seconds. It refers to time as a measurable resource. Kairos means an appointed time, an opportune moment, or a due season.

Let's think of chronos time as our lifeline and kairos time as significant events intersecting our lifeline at various points. For example, I'm walking along measuring my life in days, months, and years—chronos time—and at age seventeen, I meet Jesus. Meeting Christ was a kairos event that radically affected the rest of my life. I continue forward in chronos time, and I meet my wife. Meeting Donna was another kairos moment that altered my life forever.

All humans walking out their days in chronos time experience kairos moments.

I'm sixty-two and walking forward in my true identity, and I've experienced many amazing kairos moments in the past. But I know for certain there are more kairos moments ahead. And the kairos moments that lie ahead are going to be better than the former ones, and the former ones were amazing.

Here's an interesting thing about time and where our thinking about time is incorrect. Time doesn't move. Time doesn't pass. Time is not something you can waste or lose. Time is merely a measurement of the movement of objects in space.

Think of chronos and kairos time as the young nation of Israel is walking toward the land promised to them by God. It took Israel forty years, or 14,600 days, of chronos time to travel from Egypt to Canaan, a journey that should have taken about eleven days. So in the 14,589 "wasted" days, what part of the kairos moment did the people of Israel miss? None.

An entire generation of Israelites refused to walk into the kairos moment, but they didn't miss it because the moment passed them. They missed the kairos moment because they refused to move forward in their true identity and instead wandered around for forty years as grasshoppers with a grasshopper god.

Here is the good news. Kairos events cannot and will not pass you by when you aren't looking. It can take one day or seventy-five years, but you will arrive at these kairos moments as long as you keep walking forward in your true identity.

Here is the sad news. You do have the ability to let fear, guilt, and shame stop you from moving forward. Like the fearful Israelites, you can say no to God's kairos moments for you. Don't make that mistake.

Time is not an enemy. Created by God, time is beautiful. Time is simply measuring you walking forward into what God has for you, starting today. The apostle Paul writes, "If we live in the Spirit, let us also walk in the Spirit" (Gal. 5:25 NKJV).

No matter how old you are or whether this is the first day you have ever thought of hearing your identity or entering the kingdom of God, kairos moments are waiting for you. Jesus is right there with you saying, "Ready? Let's go." You will start walking into the appointed times for you, straight into the kingdom of God. That is the beauty of your future.

You haven't missed anything yet in your life, not one thing. God says to ask him and he'll give you the years the locusts have eaten away.[11] Ask God for the years back.

Here are some action steps.

Pay attention to God. "Lord, which way are we going? Where are you on this path? Lord, how do we go? What do you want me to know? What do you want me to do?" Then start moving forward toward a goal or destination.

What is the goal or destination? Ask God. Always seek God's wisdom.

The people you meet along the way will be keys to your future. Weird people, smart people, Christian people, non-Christian people—all are important. This is the beauty of the mystery of the other. Know everyone. Don't have enemies.

From Coward to Counselor

Some time ago, I met a man named Jerry. He was forty-five years old. He was a massive, athletic man who had just come to Christ.

As a new believer, Jerry still struggled with anger and violence. Life experiences had made him quite hostile. I started meeting with Jerry and walked with him through his challenges in his new relationship with Jesus. I asked him his story and he told me that when he was young, he was physically bigger than other kids. His dad and his neighbor said, "You ought to play rugby." The problem was he didn't want to play rugby because he wasn't mean; he was actually quite tenderhearted. Rugby, however, was important to his dad, so his dad kept making him play rugby junior league and then on into secondary school.

Every time he played, the coaches would say, "You got to get mad. You're too nice out there. You gotta get mad." Consequently, he started taking on this identity of being angry on the field because he didn't want to play in the first place. But when he got mad, he succeeded, and he received a lot of accolades. He went through high school and he was really good and he got really big and he became really mean. Therefore, he was awarded a university scholarship to play rugby, but he hated playing the game. He accepted the scholarship in order to attend university, and his identity became the big, mean, angry, rugby guy.

In his second year, he was severely injured. As a result, he couldn't play and lost his scholarship. But his scholarship status had made passing grades automatic, so he'd never had to study. Therefore, he considers himself stupid.

Now he is big and mean and not smart. He is no longer a rugby star. What is he? Big, mean, angry, and doesn't know what to do. So he fights people. He fights and he gets arrested often and he gets a girl pregnant. His life turns into a protracted, violent disaster.

Then he meets Jesus, and now he's in the kingdom of God and he's asking, "What do I do?" The anger just doesn't go away like magic, so he's asking me, "What do I do with this intense anger?"

I say, "I don't know, but I know how to know." We begin meeting and praying together.

During the prayer process, I ask the Lord to reveal to Jerry the first time he felt this level of anger in his life and what was the source of this anger.

Jerry remembered his first feeling of anger as being on the rugby field as a youth. He didn't like playing rugby, but his dad kept telling him he was weak and a coward if he didn't want to play sports. The whole scenario made Jerry feel like a disappointment to his dad. It gave him an identity of unworthiness.

There it is. Just as young David was learning how to fight lions and bears and coming into his true self, young Jerry was learning how to feel unworthy and his anger rose up to protect him and help him succeed in the false self. He takes on this false identity and begins to live it out.

Jerry's false identity of "unworthy" is the source of his pain, and that is where the Lord wants to meet him—on the day Jerry began to believe that lie. The Lord was with Jerry on that day. I ask God, "Lord, what do you want Jerry to know about that day, that time, when he felt that sense of unworthiness?"

Jerry recalled a particularly humiliating incident with his father. As we prayed through the memory, Jerry sensed the Lord saying, "I made you to be a counselor to people."

When Jerry heard this, he began to cry. This big, angry man started to cry and said, "I think God says I'm his counselor."

"What kind of counselor?" I ask.

"A family counselor."

Really? Wow. What a history for that. It makes sense. But what does the enemy want Jerry to fear and avoid? His true identity. When the Lord says, "You're my family counselor," the enemy will immediately challenge with, "Really, you? Impossible."

This is why it is so beneficial to be in a community of trusted believers when you are hearing from the Lord.

When our small group found out that God called Jerry a family counselor, we all encouraged him and held him accountable to becoming a family counselor. This is the definition of true accountability, affirming and nudging people forward in their true identity and destiny.

I asked Jerry, "How does it make you feel to know that you will be a counselor to families?"

"It makes me feel kind of good but look at my life," Jerry sadly replied.

Wrong answer. "How does it make you *feel* to know that you will be a family counselor?"

Jerry said, "It will be the most redemptive thing I could ever do or imagine."

Right answer! That is Jesus. That is what Jesus does.

Jerry is paying *attention*. Jerry is *aware* and he can hear the *annunciation* of God calling him a counselor. But look at his life; it's a wreck. It's like when Saul of Tarsus encountered the living Christ on the Damascus road and discovered that in his mother's womb he was called to rescue and defend the Gentiles. Strangely, Saul of Tarsus, now the apostle Paul, had been committed to ridding the world of Gentiles, even killing them. This is how God redeems people and events. It is such a beautiful mystery.

When Jerry said, "I feel like I'm a family counselor," we immediately affirmed him and confirmed what he heard with Scripture.

God's communication to you will be aligned with the principles and themes in Scripture. Jesus would certainly call Jerry "Counselor." Who understands family tragedy more than Jerry? Who understands anger in a family more than Jerry?

Now Jerry needs an *action* plan. To become a family counselor, he needs a university degree. God didn't have to come in a vision to tell Jerry this. It's common sense.

"Oh no!" Jerry exclaimed. "I've never passed a class in my life. I'm forty-five years old. I don't want to go into a classroom; I'm dumb. I can't even write a good sentence."

While it was true that Jerry had a terrible secondary school and university GPA, it was not true that he was dumb and couldn't perform well in academic situations. To encourage him on his journey, our community rallied around him and personally accompanied him through two years of college, where he finished with honors.

With continued support from his community, Jerry then completed his counseling degree while volunteering at his local church in the counseling program. During these years, Jerry also reconciled with his wife and children.

Although Jerry had wandered for forty-five years, lost in a false identity, the kairos moments in his life didn't pass him by; they never moved. As Jerry moved forward in his true identity, the kairos moments came into view and he walked right into them.

It doesn't matter how old you are. Your destiny and purpose are right there if you are willing to walk each day in the right direction in your true identity. Would you pray and ask God to help you right now?

> *God, help me to pay attention to who you say I am. Help me to stop believing the lies and accusations as you exchange them for your truth. Help me to be aware of what you're doing in my life and what the enemy is doing in my life. Help me to hear from you, the true Lord God. Then, Lord, would you help me to develop action steps in the direction of those things you have for me?*

This is what it means to abide in life-giving union with Christ as he abides in life-giving union with you.

Back to the Beginning

Since we began this journey together by examining an interaction between Peter and Jesus (John 6), let's finish by considering another conversation between that relentless rookie and his faithful Field Training Officer recorded in Matthew 16:15–19 (MSG).

Jesus began the conversation with a question to the entire rookie class: "Who do you say I am?"

Simon Peter said, "You're the Christ, the Messiah, the Son of the living God." *The true identity of Jesus!*

Jesus came back, "God bless you, Simon, son of Jonah! You didn't get that answer out of books or from teachers. My Father in heaven, God himself, let you in on this secret of who I really am." *A result of Peter's attention to and awareness of God the Father!*

"And now I'm going to tell you who you are, really are. You are Peter, a rock." *Jesus's annunciation of Peter's true identity!*

"This is the rock on which I will put together my church, a church so expansive with energy that not even the gates of hell will be able to keep it out." *Receive the truth!*

"And that's not all. You will have complete and free access to God's kingdom, keys to open any and every door: no more barriers between heaven and earth, earth and heaven." *Take action!*

Abiding = Attention, Awareness, Annunciation, and Action.

Got it? Then let's go.

Notes

Preface

1. Art (nmn) Blumfield, a legendary figure in the field of counterterrorism, was my mentor and always introduced himself using the abbreviation "nmn" which is short for no-middle-name. Out of respect, I introduce him here as he requested. Also, I'm pretty sure it's not his real name. I'll probably never know his real name.

2. Exod. 1:15–21.

Introduction

1. One evening, after having consumed several pints, the Troll explained that his fondness for the word *abide* originated with his Irish Catholic mother, who recited it nightly as part of a prayer. He did also love *The Big Lebowski* in which the term *abides* is used more than twenty times.

2. James 1:19.

3. From this point on, for the sake of space, the reader may feel free to insert pretty much any vulgar term, pretty much anywhere in any statement made by the Troll, and be pretty much accurate.

4. John 15.

5. John Piper, "What Does It Mean to 'Abide in Christ'?," September 22, 2017, in *Ask Pastor John*, podcast, MP3 audio, 12:16, https://www.desiring god.org/interviews/what-does-it-mean-to-abide-in-christ.

6. John 15:1, 5, 7, 8, 9, 11, 26.

7. John 15:14.

8. John 16:13–14.

9. John 3:16–17.

10. Throughout our time together, you may come up with a descriptive nickname for me, but please keep it to yourself.

11. Merriam-Webster defines *annunciation* as "the act of announcing or of being announced." When referring to the words spoken by God/Christ/

Spirit, I like the sacredness of the term *annunciation* as it pertains to him announcing his will to us. *Merriam-Webster.com Dictionary*, s.v. "annunciation," accessed November 16, 2021, https://www.merriam-webster.com/dictionary/annunciation.

Part 1 Attention

1. David Garrison, "Muslims Turning to Christ—A Global Phenomenon," *Premier Christianity*, May 11, 2016, https://www.premierchristianity.com/home/muslims-turning-to-christ-a-global-phenomenon/2056.article.
2. Isa. 6.
3. Nick Pappas's story is also detailed in Philip Caputo, *A Rumor of War* (New York: Owl Books, 1977).
4. Heb. 2:14–18.
5. Rom. 5.
6. James 5:16.
7. Gen. 3.

Part 2 Awareness

1. Joseph Chilton Pearce, *The Biology of Transcendence: A Blueprint of the Human Spirit* (Rochester, VT: Park Street Press, 2002), 111–45; Joseph Chilton Pierce; *The Heart-Mind Matrix: How the Heart Can Teach the Mind New Ways to Think* (Rochester, VT: Park Street Press, 2012); Steve Edwards, "Heart Intelligence: Heuristic Phenomenological Investigation into the Coherence Experience Using HeartMath Methods," Springer Link, October 17, 2017, https:/link.springer.com/article/10.1007/s00146-017-0767-7.
2. Receiving identity from God in community protects us from the counterfeit of radical individualism, which is self-generated, subjective, and produces internal and external conflict.
3. James 4:7.
4. 1 Sam. 17:12.
5. 1 Sam. 16:23.
6. Heb. 12:2.
7. 1 Sam. 30:1–6.
8. Isa. 26:3.
9. Luke 19:1–10.
10. Matt. 12:38–45; Luke 11:16–36.

Part 3 Annunciation

1. Ps. 115:5; Isa. 44:10; 1 Cor. 12:2.
2. See also Arthur Koestler, *The Act of Creation* (London: Hutchinson and Company, 1964), for an even more comprehensive *"eureka"* study with a similar conclusion.
3. Matt. 3:17.
4. Luke 4:14.

5. Matt. 7:7–11.

6. Luke 3:21; 5:15–16; 6:12; 9:18, 29; 10:17–21.

7. Matt. 6:5–7.

8. Matt. 6:8.

9. C. S. Lewis, *The Lion, the Witch and the Wardrobe* (New York: Harper-Collins Publishers, 1950), 146.

10. This is not his real name.

11. See the Chalcedonian Creed (AD 451), https://www.trinityfay.org/wp-content/uploads/The-Chalcedonian-Creed.pdf.

12. Martin Luther, "Theses Concerning Faith and Law" (1535), American Edition 34:112, https://therebelgod.com/Luther/.

13. For examples in early Christianity, see Charles A. Gieschen, *Angelomorphic Christology: Antecedents and Early Evidence* (Leiden: Brill, 1998); and Charles A. Gieschen, "The Real Presence of the Son before Christ," *Concordia Theological Quarterly* 68, no. 2 (April 2004): 105–26, http://www.ctsfw.net/media/pdfs/gieschenrealpresence.pdf.

14. Martin Luther, "Treatise on the Last Words of David" (1543), American Edition 15:313–14, https://therebelgod.com/Luther/.

15. Exod. 3:14. God further refers to himself as "I am the God of your father, the God of Abraham, the God of Isaac and the God of Jacob" (Exod. 3:6 NIV).

16. Exod. 33:11.

17. Tim Mackie, "What is the Shema: Learning to Listen To and Love God," *BibleProject* (blog), accessed November 16, 2021, https://bibleproject.com/blog/what-is-the-shema/.

18. Exod. 2:12.

19. Exod. 3:1, Hebrew אַחַר, Blue Letter Bible, accessed September 9, 2021, https://www.blueletterbible.org/lexicon/h310/kjv/wlc/0-1/.

20. Exod. 4:14.

21. Søren Kierkegaard, *The Sickness Unto Death* (Milwaukee: Wiseblood Classics, 2013), chapter 1.

22. David G. Benner, *The Gift of Being Yourself: The Sacred Call to Self-Discovery* (Downers Grove, IL: InterVarsity, 2015), 83.

23. See St. Augustine's Tractate 15 on the Gospel of John, Section 5, https://www.newadvent.org/fathers/1701015.htm.

24. Read the book of Nehemiah for a case study in this historical hostility.

25. John 4:11–12.

26. *Memar Marqah*, 4.7, 12.

27. *Memar Marqah*, 6.3.

28. *Memar Marqah*, 2.1.

29. *Memar Marqah*, 4.12.

30. In the Orthodox Church, the Samaritan woman is remembered as St. Photini, martyred by Nero for her unrelenting preaching of the gospel.

31. Ann Voskamp, *One Thousand Gifts: A Dare to Live Fully Right Where You Are* (Nashville: W Publishing Group, 2010), 167.

32. 1 Sam. 27:1.

33. 1 Cor. 4:1.

34. The term *ephod* in the Old Testament refers to two different things. One is the garment worn by the high priest; the other seems to be a transportable idol (1 Sam. 30:7).

35. Rom. 5:20.

36. 1 Sam. 23:1–3, 4–5, 10–11, 12–14; 30:8–9; 2 Sam. 2:1–2; 5:17–21, 22–25; 21:1.

37. Matt. 16:22.

38. Rom. 12:1–2.

Part 4 Action

1. Floyd Nolen Jones, *The Chronology of the Old Testament* (Green Forest, AR: Master Books, 2005), 99–100.

2. Exod. 1:21.

3. Heb. 11:24–28.

4. Dan. 1.

5. Dan. 1:3.

6. John 16:7.

7. Brené Brown, "Shame v. Guilt," *Brené Brown* (blog), January 14, 2013, https://brenebrown.com/blog/2013/01/14/shame-v-guilt/.

8. Isa. 28:16; Zeph. 3:19; Rom. 10:11.

9. 2 Sam. 11.

10. Naomi Breslau, Edward L. Peterson, and Lonni R. Schultz, "A Second Look at Prior Trauma and the Posttraumatic Stress Disorder Effects of Subsequent Trauma: A Prospective Epidemiological Study," *Archives of General Psychiatry* 65, no. 4 (April 2008): 431–37, https://pubmed.ncbi.nlm.nih.gov/18391131/.

11. Joel 2:25.

Jamie Winship is a former Metro DC area police officer who spent nearly thirty years living and working in the Muslim world, teaching people how to hear from God and live in his kingdom. Jamie and his wife, Donna, speak around the United States and across the globe to help people find their God-given identity and experience a life of freedom. Jamie and Donna live in East Tennessee. Learn more at IdentityExchange.com.

Transformed individuals
transforming communities.

www.identityexchange.com

Connect with
Jamie

 **identityexchange**

thejamiewinship

Identity Exchange

One-on-One Online Identity Coaching